CROSSING BORDERS

SHARING JOURNEYS

Effective capacity building with immigrant and refugee groups

NEXUS PROJECT REPORT

Lead writer:

Sarah Gleason

Contributors:

Emil Angelica
Vicki Asakura
Hilary Binder-Aviles
Barbara W. Fane
Anushka Fernandopulle
Cheryl Hamilton
Monica Herrera
Barbara Jeanetta
Sida Ly-Xiong

Amanuel Melles
Heba Nimr
Ann Philbin
Anne Pyke
Charley Ravine
Monica Regan
Luz Rodriguez
Alfredo Vergara-Lobo

Fieldstone Alliance is committed to strengthening the performance of the nonprofit sector. Through the synergy of its consulting, training, publishing, and research and demonstration projects, Fieldstone Alliance provides solutions to issues facing non-profits, funders, and the communities they serve. Fieldstone Alliance was formerly Wilder Publishing and Wilder Consulting departments of the Amherst H. Wilder Foundation. If you would like more information about Fieldstone Alliance and our services, please visit www.FieldstoneAlliance.org.

We hope you find this book useful! For information about other Fieldstone Alliance publications, please contact:

Fieldstone Alliance Publishing Center
60 Plato Boulevard East
Suite 150
Saint Paul, MN 55107
800-274-6024

Edited by Vincent Hyman
Text designed by Kirsten Nielsen

First printing, July 2006

Nexus

The Nexus Project was funded by a grant from the W. K. Kellogg Foundation. For more information about the Nexus Project, visit www.FieldstoneAlliance.org.

CONTENTS

EXECUTIVE SUMMARY

Background

Immigration to North America has increased significantly in recent decades, both in absolute numbers and in percentage of the population. Mexico, Central America, and the Caribbean are the source of more than half of the immigrants in the United States, while Europe and Asia provide the bulk of immigrants to Canada. Immigrants come to North America from all corners of the earth, driven by economic forces, flight from war and conflict, or reunification with family members.

A growing number of nonprofit organizations have been created by immigrants and refugees to serve their communities in North America. These immigrant- and refugee-led organizations (IRLOs) work to provide services and meet a variety of needs, while at the same time building the infrastructure of these communities. Capacity builders have a special opportunity and responsibility to provide appropriate and effective services to IRLOs. The Nexus Project was created to help meet this challenge.

This is the final report of the Nexus Project. Through a grant from the W. K. Kellogg Foundation Innovation Fund, Fieldstone Alliance initiated the two-year project in January 2004. The goal of Nexus was to enhance the knowledge and skills of capacity builders across North America in working with immigrant- and refugee-led organizations. The Nexus Project had two main components: research on capacity building with IRLOs and formation of a peer learning community among those who build the capacity of these organizations.

Research

Wilder Research Center was hired to review the literature on capacity building with IRLOs, to interview IRLOs that had undertaken capacity building activities, and to interview capacity building providers. A separate document, *Factors in Successful Capacity Building with Immigrant- and Refugee-Led Organizations*, contains findings from the research. A summary can be found in Appendix 1 of this report.

Peer learning community

The Nexus Project brought together eleven capacity building organizations that work with IRLOs in North America:

- Center to Support Immigrant Organizing (CSIO), Boston, MA

- Community Consulting Group (formerly part of Wilder Center for Communities), Minneapolis, MN

- CompassPoint Nonprofit Services, San Francisco, CA

- Fieldstone Alliance, Inc. (formerly part of Wilder Center for Communities), St. Paul, MN

- Lutheran Immigration and Refugee Service (RefugeeWorks), Baltimore, MD

- Management Assistance Program (MAP) for Nonprofits, St. Paul, MN

- Mosaica: The Center for Nonprofit Development and Pluralism, Washington, DC

- Nonprofit Assistance Center (NAC), Seattle, WA

- Partnership for Immigrant Leadership and Action (PILA), San Francisco, CA

- Twin Cities Local Initiatives Support Corporation (LISC), St. Paul, MN

- United Way of Greater Toronto, Canada

Over the course of two years, representatives of the Nexus partner organizations shared resources through monthly conference calls and convened for three two-day gatherings.

Seven Effectiveness Factors

A group of seven broad factors that contribute to effective capacity building with IRLOs emerged from the collective experience of the Nexus partners, research interviews, and the learning community process. These "enabling factors" for capacity building practitioners are

1. **Relevant experience and knowledge**
   The capacity builder has experience and knowledge that is relevant to the particular IRLO, the kind of work it does, the community the IRLO serves, the particular challenge or opportunity to be addressed, and other elements of the organization's context.

2. **Cultural competence**
   The capacity builder has the ability to function and perform effectively in the cross-cultural situations encountered.

3. **Mutual relationship**
   The capacity builder builds a mutual, trusting relationship with the IRLO.

4. **Client-centered and asset-based approaches**
   The capacity building approach and methods are designed to meet the IRLO's specific needs and self-defined goals, and build on the organization's specific assets.

5. **Participatory methods**
   Participatory methods are used to actively engage IRLO stakeholders in planning and implementing capacity building work.

6. **Peer learning**
   Opportunities to learn from and with peers are included in the capacity building process.

7. **Leadership development**
   The development of leadership knowledge and skills is integrated into the capacity building process.

Lessons Learned

This report draws three broad lessons for the capacity building field, with implications for the funding community, IRLOs, and capacity builders.

1. Effective capacity building takes time, which requires resources.

2. More immigrant and refugee capacity builders are needed.

3. Capacity builders need continuous learning and development.

How to Use This Report

This report includes the following sections:

The Introduction describes the formation of the Nexus Project, its goals, and its working definitions.

Chapter 1 describes the factors that result in effective capacity building with immigrant- and refugee-led organizations. This chapter will help capacity builders better understand the skills needed to succeed in this work.

Chapter 2 presents case studies from each of the Nexus partners. Each case study illustrates a practice used by Nexus partners when working with IRLOs and highlights principles that other capacity builders can apply when working with similar groups.

Chapter 3 details lessons Nexus partners learned through the course of this project. It further states implications of these lessons for those who fund work with IRLOs, for IRLO leaders, and for capacity building providers. It also suggests lessons for peer learning related to work with IRLOs.

The Appendices include a summary of IRLO research conducted by Wilder Research Center specifically for Nexus; a bibliography; and descriptions of the organizations and individuals who contributed to this report.

INTRODUCTION

OUR SHARED JOURNEY

I mmigration to North America has increased significantly in recent decades, both in absolute numbers and in percentage of the population.

In March 2005, there were 35.2 million immigrants and refugees (total foreign-born population) in the United States, the highest number ever recorded. They account for 12.1 percent of the total U.S. population, the highest percentage in eight decades. If current trends continue, within a decade this percentage will surpass the high of 14.7 percent reached in 1910, at the peak of the last great wave of immigration.[1] Mexico, Central America, and the Caribbean are the source of more than half of the immigrants in the United States, while Europe and Asia provide the bulk of immigrants to Canada. Immigrants come to North America from all corners of the earth, driven by economic forces, flight from war and conflict, or reunification with family members.

A growing number of nonprofit organizations have been created by immigrants and refugees to serve their communities in North America. These immigrant- and refugee-led organizations (IRLOs) work to provide services and meet a variety of needs, while at the same time building the infrastructure of these communities. IRLOs provide a venue and opportunity for immigrant and refugee leaders to build their skills, experience, and connections, and a vehicle for building the collective power of immigrant communities.

Capacity builders have a special opportunity and responsibility to provide appropriate and effective services to IRLOs. The Nexus Project was created to help meet this challenge.

---

[1] Steven Camarota, *Immigrants at Mid-Decade: A Snapshot of America's Foreign-Born Population in 2005* (Center for Immigration Studies, December 2005), 1.

The Nexus Project

The Nexus Project was a two-year initiative funded by the W. K. Kellogg Foundation. Nexus included eleven partners, all capacity building organizations with extensive experience working with immigrant- and refugee-led organizations. As partners, we had two related purposes:

1. To strengthen our own capacity building practice with IRLOs

2. To use our learning to strengthen the field of capacity building with IRLOs

The initiative included three face-to-face meetings and a series of conference calls. During these encounters, we built relationships, shared resources, and learned from one another in a variety of ways. We also contracted with Wilder Research Center to review the literature on capacity building with IRLOs. We worked with the researchers to design and implement two sets of research interviews—one set with IRLOs that had undertaken capacity building activities and one set with capacity building providers—to learn more about our own work with IRLOs from multiple perspectives.[2]

We came together from cities on the East and West Coasts of the United States, and from Toronto, Canada, to meet with others working in Minnesota. In the beginning, it seemed as if we had little in common, other than experience working with IRLOs. Our organizations and our work—the "what," the "why," and the "how" of it—are diverse. But we share a common passion and devotion to our work, and we were committed to using this opportunity both to strengthen our own practice and to share our learning with others. Though our progress was bumpy and there is much that, in hindsight, many of us wish we had done differently, we all benefited. Along the way we learned more about what we have in common and found that, collectively, we have something important to offer our colleagues. That "something" is contained in this document.

Crossing borders, becoming partners

Nexus partners have diverse goals, values, programmatic approaches, and funding sources. The Nexus Project began with a focus on *organizational* capacity building, but at our first gathering we discovered that many Nexus partners don't separate community and leader capacity building from organizational capacity building. The range of our interventions and practices is very broad, and this made finding common ground difficult.

---

[2]   The Wilder Research Center report is titled *Factors in Successful Capacity Building with Immigrant- and Refugee-Led Organizations* and is available on the Fieldstone Alliance web site at www.FieldstoneAlliance.org/refugee_report.cfm. A summary of the report is contained in Appendix 1 of this document.

Among the Nexus partner organizations are two national nonprofit management service organizations, a local nonprofit management service organization, and a local for-profit consulting group. These organizations provide a mix of capacity building services to a broad range of clients, either on a fee-for-service basis, or in third-party-funded initiatives. One partner offers a similar range of capacity building services, but focuses on its local communities of color in order to empower those communities. Another partner with a similar goal operates nationally. Two partner organizations, on opposite coasts, work specifically to support immigrant organizing. One partner works exclusively with organizations providing U.S. government-funded employment services to refugees. Another provides funding and technical assistance to community development corporations locally, including some that are IRLOs. And one Nexus organization, our only Canadian partner, is primarily a funding organization, represented in the Nexus Project by staff from its strong capacity building division. (To learn more about each organization, see Nexus Partner Organizations, pages 81–84.)

Despite many differences, all of the Nexus partner organizations share a commitment to building the capacity of IRLOs. We live in an interconnected world with sharp disparities in wealth and opportunity among nations and violent conflicts ongoing across the globe. These conditions—often a result of the policies of our own governments—are among the forces driving people from their home countries. The immigrant and refugee communities in the United States and Canada will continue to grow. All of the Nexus partners are committed to the important work of building the capacity of IRLOs to serve and strengthen their own communities.

The individuals who participated as representatives of the partner organizations come from a variety of backgrounds and play different roles in their work with IRLOs. Some of us are from immigrant or refugee backgrounds, though most of us are not. Most of us who are *not* immigrant-identified are White. Nearly all of us have extensive personal and professional experience in immigrant and refugee communities. The majority of us are women. (See Authors of This Report, pages 85–88 for more information.)

A shared learning journey

As we worked together, we found that we have different relationships with IRLOs, and use different language when talking about our work with them. Some of us came to Nexus steeped in the capacity building field using language typical of consultants. Others of us were immersed in specific kinds of technical assistance and not sure what we had to offer to our colleagues doing other kinds of work. Still others were steeped in community organizing and popular education[3] approaches that have recently been recognized as part of the capacity building universe.[4]

From the beginning of the Nexus Project, we had more questions than answers. For example, what did each of us mean by the term capacity building? What about "success?" What would be our common definition of "immigrant- and refugee-led organization?" What is the relationship between capacity building and community organizing? Ultimately we answered *some* of these questions, but conversations remain to be finished.

Many of us wanted to spend more time exploring the idea of cultural competence, articulating what it means to act as an ally, and understanding how the different underlying values shape our work. Some of us wonder what we would have learned if we had talked more about the goals of our work. We also wonder how the conversation would have been different if more of us were from immigrant or refugee backgrounds, or if we had engaged immigrant and refugee leaders more in the process.

Even amidst the open questions, we found it nourishing to be engaged with our far-flung colleagues through this project. Each organization gained new perspectives on its own work, and how that work fits into the breadth of the capacity building field. We learned that we are part of a very dynamic field, and that our colleagues have lots of ideas, approaches, and practices that we can learn from. We saw each other being creative in doing capacity building, confirming our belief that our work cannot be formulaic—there is no cookie-cutter approach to working with immigrant- and refugee-led organizations. We also sharpened our awareness of the many ways the local, national, and global political context shapes our work. The perspectives, experiences, tools, and relationships we shared will continue to strengthen our work into the future.

---

[3] *Popular education* is a form of adult education that invites participants to critically examine their lives and take action to change social conditions. It emphasizes collective problem solving, participation, critical reflection, shared leadership, and the value of participants' life experiences and concerns.

[4] Tom Backer, Jane Ellen Bleeg, and Kathryn Groves, *The Expanding Universe: New Directions in Nonprofit Capacity Building* (Washington, DC: Alliance for Nonprofit Management, 2004).

DEFINITIONS WE USED

We could not proceed with our work without developing some shared definitions. We used the following.

Immigrant- and refugee-led organizations (IRLOs)

IRLOs share the following characteristics:

- The executive director or senior leadership roles are held by refugees or immigrants

- Refugees or immigrants hold 51 percent of the board of directors

- Refugees or immigrants constitute 51 percent of the people served

- The constituency faces issues related to poverty, lack of access to power, and lack of resources

- They are *either* incorporated *or* have a fiscal sponsor

Note: Evolving IRLOs may not currently meet all criteria, but are working toward them.

Capacity

The ability of nonprofit organizations to fulfill their missions in an effective manner.[5]

Capacity building

Activities that strengthen a nonprofit and help it better fulfill its mission,[6] usually by building leadership, strategic positioning, programmatic effectiveness, external relationships, management functioning, and financial stability.

Immigrant

A person who has left one country to settle in another country, or a person who identifies himself or herself as a member of an immigrant community.

Refugee

For the purposes of our work, a refugee is a person who identifies herself or himself as a refugee. The United Nations defines a refugee as a person who "owing to a well-founded fear of being persecuted for reasons of race, religion, nationality, membership of a particular social group, or political opinion, is outside the country of his nationality, and is unable to or, owing to such fear, is unwilling to avail himself of the protection of that country...."[7] The legal determination of refugee status, however, is up to national governments. In the United States, this process has often reflected political priorities and led to glaring injustices. There are certain protections and benefits that accompany legal status as a refugee.

[5] Alison De Lucca, *Rising with the Tide: Capacity Building Strategies for Small, Emerging Minority Organizations* (Los Angeles Immigrant Funders' Collaborative, 2002) 10.

[6] Paul Connolly and Carol Lukas, *Strengthening Nonprofit Performance: A Funder's Guide to Capacity Building* (Saint Paul, MN: Fieldstone Alliance, 2002) 19.

[7] United Nations High Commissioner for Refugees, *The State of the World's Refugees 2000* (Cambridge, MA: Oxford University Press, January 2001) 23.

Our Goal for You

In this report, we present a small taste of what we have learned through our own work with IRLOs and through the Nexus Project. We distill some factors that we believe contribute to effective capacity building with IRLOs, and we share some examples of how we implement these factors in our own work. We also draw lessons for our colleagues in capacity building, including funders and IRLOs, along with some questions that we believe are ripe for further exploration. We look forward to continuing the conversation and the journey. We hope you will join us.

I mmigrant- and refugee-led organizations (IRLOs), as defined in this project, are quite diverse with a few elements in common.[8]

While they are all led by immigrants or refugees and have a constituency that faces issues related to poverty and lack of access to power and resources, everything else about them varies. They come in every size and shape imaginable. They include advocacy groups challenging government policies, and established agencies providing services through government contracts. Some are multi-ethnic, while others represent a specific constituency. These and other differences impact our capacity building work with them, as does who *we* are—in particular, whether we have a background similar to those we are working with.

The following characteristics apply to all or many IRLOs, and affect our work with them.

IRLOs are embedded in distinct communities, with distinct histories, while working within the North American community and context.

> These complex dynamics impact them and their work. We have seen, for example, the impact on IRLOs of clan rivalries, of home country politics, and of U.S. policies that affect particular immigrant groups.
>
> **Implications for capacity builders:** As capacity builders, we must be aware of these histories and dynamics, be on the lookout for their impact on the organization and on the capacity building process, and adapt our work accordingly. We must also be aware of the culture and language of the communities involved. If they are not our own communities, we need to actively learn about them.

---

[8] See our formal definition, page 11.

IRLOs and IRLO leaders often have strong community connections, a strong sense of community, and a responsibility to their community.

IRLOs can play a special role as a space for associational life—community centers and sites of civic engagement. IRLO leaders are also community leaders, often responsible to the community "24-7." An immigrant executive director gets requests, feedback, support, and criticism not just at the office, but from friends and family wherever he or she goes—at home, the grocery store, gatherings, and religious services.

Implications for capacity builders: Traditional models of organizational structure and governance may not apply. Roles in the organization may be quite fluid. IRLO leaders have competing demands for their time and attention. Capacity building work may be affected by events in the community.

IRLOs are embedded in communities with less institutional power than the dominant community, less knowledge of the nonprofit sector and institutional norms, and less access to systems and resources important to nonprofits.

In this way IRLOs are like other organizations with marginalized constituencies, such as those that serve youth or African Americans.

Implications for capacity builders: It is critical that we be aware of our own power and pay attention to power dynamics and differentials. There are many ways as capacity builders that we can act as allies, transferring knowledge and facilitating access to systems and resources.

IRLOs often play important roles in building the capacity of their own communities.

Board, staff, and volunteer roles with IRLOs offer significant opportunities for immigrants and refugees to build their individual and collective skills and power.

Implications for capacity builders: We know that for many IRLOs, building community capacity is an important outcome of building organizational capacity. This heightens the importance of broad and deep engagement in organizational capacity building efforts, and of leadership development, especially the development of leaders among the IRLOs' constituents. Further, outsiders may perceive the IRLO as a reflection of and representative of the entire population it serves—so if the IRLO appears to be struggling, people from outside the community may assume that the whole population is struggling. This puts an undue burden of representation on the IRLO, as compared to an organization not identified with a particular community. Capacity builders need to be aware of the double burden and of the inferences others may draw from their presence.

Many IRLOs are small, emerging, and under-resourced, and many are addressing multiple pressing—even overwhelming—community needs.

IRLOs are also often in flux because of changing circumstances. The confluence of stressors presents many challenges for capacity builders, though they are not unique to IRLOs. Many IRLOs and IRLO leaders have not used capacity building services before, or have not had good experience with them.

Implications for capacity builders: We have a responsibility to meet IRLOs where they are and support them in clarifying their needs and their goals.

Some IRLOs and IRLO leaders and communities operate most effectively in languages other than English.

Even those who are fluent in English may be able to participate more effectively in their home languages.

Implications for capacity builders: This means that we may need to invest more effort, time, and money to communicate in the IRLO's preferred language or across linguistic differences. When we work in English, we need to be aware of our language and watch out for terms, idioms, or metaphors that don't translate well.

Practitioner Effectiveness Factors

From our combined experience, from our research interviews, and from our own conversations, themes emerged about what it takes to build the capacity of IRLOs. We distilled these themes into what we initially called "success factors." That title, though, implies a shared definition of success and more empirical data than is currently available. So, we call them *effectiveness factors.* They are the factors that we have found contribute to effectiveness in capacity building with IRLOs. These factors are supported by our own experience in the field, as well as by the findings of the Nexus Project research.

These factors specifically concern our colleagues—practitioners who do the work of capacity building. This includes staff of management service organizations, consultants, technical assistance providers, facilitators, and others. Our factors address **who** practitioners are; **what** they bring in terms of skills, experience, attitudes, and values; and **how** they do their work with IRLOs. The factors are

1. Relevant experience and knowledge
2. Cultural competence
3. Mutual relationship
4. Client-centered and asset-based approach
5. Participatory methods
6. Peer learning
7. Leadership development

1. Relevant experience and knowledge

The capacity builder has experience and knowledge that is relevant to the particular IRLO, the kind of work it does, the community the IRLO serves, the particular challenge or opportunity to be addressed, and other elements of the organization's context.

A capacity builder's own cultural identities, as well his or her personal and social experiences, contribute to this knowledge and experience base. Relevant professional experience includes past work with organizations that are similar to the IRLO the person is currently working with. Relevant organizational similarities include size, structure, mission, values, field of work, community served, developmental aspirations, and so forth. Professional knowledge should include an understanding of the particular institutional, political, and funding environment affecting the IRLO. Relevant experience may also include the contracted consultancy's "bench strength"—the capacity to switch out consultants for a better fit.

2. Cultural competence

The capacity builder has the ability to function and perform effectively in the cross-cultural situations encountered.

Cultural competence includes the capacity builder's relative cultural "fluency" in the particular cultures involved, as well as her or his ability to bridge (work across and connect) cultures. The development of cultural competence is an ongoing, intentional process. Elements of cultural competency for a capacity builder include

- Self-awareness and honesty with others regarding one's own identity, culture, values, and power (or access to power)
- The ability to acquire and integrate cultural knowledge, including the power dynamics within the organization and community, and its history and socio-economic circumstances
- The ability to bridge language and cultural differences
- The ability to adapt one's practice to diverse cultural contexts

3. Mutual relationship

The capacity builder builds a mutual, trusting relationship with the IRLO.

Mutual relationships are crucial when working with immigrant- and refugee-led organizations. The quality of the relationship is very often the key factor in capacity building. The best relationships are built on mutual respect, power sharing, and reciprocal learning. In this kind of a relationship, the IRLO feels valued by the capacity builder, and the capacity builder acts as an ally for the IRLO. Such relationships can only be developed with a significant investment of time, integrity, and authentic engagement.

4. Client-centered and asset-based approaches

The capacity building approach and methods are designed to meet the IRLO's specific needs and self-defined goals, and to build on its specific assets.

The IRLO must drive and direct the capacity building process. Capacity builders need to be flexible in their approaches in order to meet IRLOs where they're at and to adapt to changing IRLO circumstances. The best approaches build on existing strengths and assets at the individual, organizational, cultural, and community level. Capacity building methods and tools must be customized to the IRLO's specific needs and context.

5. Participatory methods

Participatory methods are used to actively engage IRLO stakeholders in planning and implementing capacity building work.

Participatory methods draw on and reinforce the knowledge, skills, and experiences of participants. Using participatory methods for processes such as assessment, planning, and evaluation uncovers better information and creates broader ownership. Participatory methods also develop the IRLO's capacity to learn, adapt, and implement capacity building processes on its own in the future. Experiential and cooperative approaches are most effective for skill building and can help to bridge language and cultural differences in learning.

6. Peer learning

Opportunities to learn from and with peers are included in the capacity building process.

Peer learning strategies, including mentoring, coaching, peer exchanges, learning circles, and networking, can have significant impact. They build capacity on multiple levels. Because the question of who is a peer is crucial and can be complicated, participants should be involved in the design of peer learning strategies. Participants can learn from peers both within their own organization and across organizations and communities.

7. Leadership development

The development of leadership knowledge and skills is integrated into the capacity building process.

The intentional development of leadership has a special importance in capacity building with IRLOs. This includes engaging and developing the ownership and leadership of IRLO staff and board members throughout the process. It also includes paying attention to the cultivation and development of constituent leadership. This supports the key role that IRLOs play in developing the capacity and power of their communities.

Putting the Factors into Practice

In order for IRLOs to effectively engage in capacity building work with capacity builders, they need adequate **time, resources**, and **desire for change**.

Time

Effective capacity building takes time—both in terms of the time demand on IRLO personnel, and in terms of the duration of the engagement. Time is in short supply for IRLOs, which are often under-resourced and responding to multiple community needs. Capacity building is a long-term process that must be sustained to be effective.

Implications for capacity builders: We must be clear with IRLOs about the time they will need to invest. Our plans and timelines must be flexible. Some capacity builders limit their work to longer term (one year or longer) initiatives, or put a higher priority on longer term capacity building work.

Resources

"Time is money" in North America, which means that IRLOs need to have funding that is not tied to programming in order to support capacity building. They need money both to pay for capacity building services and to "buy" the time of their own personnel.

Implications for capacity builders: We can support IRLOs in mobilizing sufficient resources and time for capacity building. This may mean providing some services free or on a sliding scale basis, helping IRLOs locate and apply for funding, or providing stipends or mini-grants to support capacity building. Some capacity builders act as funders or intermediaries, providing more substantial support.

Desire for change

There must be adequate desire for change among those able to implement change inside the IRLO. Capacity building involves change, which is never easy. The energy to plan and implement changes must be sustained over time.

Implications for capacity builders: We must look for the desire for change within IRLO leadership, and work with champions within the organization to ensure that other people invest in the success of the capacity building initiative. To this end, we can form capacity building teams or committees that engage a cross section of IRLO stakeholders. We should create and sign agreements, contracts, or work plans with key stakeholders and identify who in the IRLO will keep others informed.

Nexus partners use a wide range of practices to effectively build the capacity of IRLOs. Many of our best practices address multiple factors. In Chapter 2 we present some of these in more detail. Here, we provide a brief introduction to a variety of Nexus partner practices that can be categorized within two of the effectiveness factors, *cultural competence* and *mutual relationship*. These two factors were often at the center of our discussions. They also are two factors where the Nexus process yielded the greatest variety of practices to share with our colleagues. Note that not all of these practices are used by all Nexus partners, nor is this list exhaustive. We hope it will spark thoughts about your own practice.

Cultural competence

[*The capacity builder has the ability to function and perform effectively in the cross-cultural situations encountered.*]

The following are the kinds of practices used by the Nexus partners to ensure cultural competency:

- *Intentional use of practitioners who are of the same culture or very familiar with the culture.* Nexus partners recognize that practitioners who share an identity or identities with the IRLO or IRLO leaders, or those who have considerable personal or professional experience with the particular cultures involved, will likely have greater cultural "fluency" in a given situation. Many Nexus partners intentionally recruit multicultural staff as well as staff who are refugees and immigrants. Nexus partners also create "consultant pools" of multicultural, refugee, and immigrant providers. Many of us work in teams—with colleagues or partner organizations—that pair practitioners who come from or know particular refugee or immigrant communities with others who do not. Others work to identify and build the capacity of capacity builders from refugee and immigrant communities.

- *Intentional development of cross-cultural communication skills.* Capacity builders who bring important experience or knowledge but are not fluent in a particular culture need to be able to communicate or transfer their expertise effectively. The ability to adapt one's practice to diverse cultural contexts is a crucial skill for all practitioners. Nexus partners seek opportunities to develop this ability through cross-cultural partnerships and by soliciting and incorporating cross-cultural input and feedback. We look for multiple ways of communicating, including visuals, participatory tools, and stories. We are also conscious of our language, particularly the metaphors and jargon that some of us use regularly. We use plain language, but also explain relevant technical terminology that IRLOs need to know. We also recruit and retain bilingual practitioners, provide language interpretation, and/or provide services and materials in appropriate languages.

- *Commitment to ongoing learning.* When we are working with IRLOs that represent cultures other than our own, we learn as much as we can about the community—its culture, history, norms, and experiences. We do this through various means, such as intake or pre-contracting discussions, organizational profiles created through conversation, site visits, and assessment processes that include questions about context. We also participate in relevant professional networks to learn about issues and context in countries of origin and here.

- *Incorporating the IRLO's and community's experience into our work.* Some Nexus partners make discussion and analysis of the immigrant and refugee experience and realities an explicit part of their work with IRLOs. For example, we may use training and tools that help IRLOs understand the context of immigration; issues they face here; political, economic, and legal structures that impact them; relevant history and context of the United States and Canada; and how change happens here. These include interactive timeline exercises and discussion of relevant videos.[9] We may also incorporate some form of information gathering with the IRLO's constituent community, such as community needs or community assets assessment.

- *Encouraging practitioner self-awareness and reflection.* Nexus partners work to continually increase our own awareness of our identities, cultures, values, biases, perspectives, and power, both as individuals and as organizations. As individuals, many of us maintain strong ties with our own cultures of origin, regularly participate in community events, and intentionally pursue work in immigrant and refugee communities and even relevant countries of origin. At an organizational level, we allow time for staff sharing and discussion around issues of culture and identity. Nexus partners also engage in strategic planning to clarify and make explicit our values and theory of change.

As practitioners, not only do we examine and reflect on our own identities, but also on our role and power as capacity builders. We are aware of the way in which we enter an organization, the "hat" we are wearing, the power it may confer, and how those factors may be perceived. We recognize that definitions of capacity, purpose of capacity building, roles of organizations and leaders, and preferred organizational structures are among the areas where we must be aware of our own perspectives, be alert for differences, and work to create clarity or mutual understanding.

---

9   Eunice Hyunhye Cho, et al., *Bridge: Building a Race and Immigration Dialogue in the Global Economy* (Oakland, CA: National Network for Immigrant and Refugee Rights, 2004) 39, 126.

- *Sharing identities and values with IRLOs.* Nexus partners find that being transparent about our own cultural identities and organizational values is an important part of building trust. We share our own stories and are explicit about our organizations' values, goals, and philosophy as we work with IRLOs.

Mutual relationship

[*The capacity builder creates a mutual, trusting relationship with the immigrant- and refugee-led organization.*]

The quality of the relationship is very often the key factor in capacity building with IRLOs. The best relationships are built on mutual respect, power sharing, and reciprocal learning. Following are the kinds of practices used by the Nexus partners to build mutual relationships:

- *Being accessible.* To build relationships, the capacity builder needs to be available and accessible to the IRLO—so much so that some Nexus partners hold accessibility as a core value in their work. A flexible schedule, accessible office location, and drop-in capability are used to increase access for IRLOs.

- *Building personal relationships with IRLOs.* Getting to know our IRLO partners personally is important, even before capacity building work begins. This requires sharing personal information, experiences, and meals. Nexus partners try to get to know IRLO leaders apart from their "work" selves, by listening, inquiring (as appropriate), and *caring* about personal information. We use introductions to begin working or learning sessions. IRLO events offer other opportunities build personal relationships outside of work settings.

- *Long-term relationship building.* It takes a significant investment of time to build a high-quality relationship. Many Nexus partners have built relationships with IRLOs and IRLO leaders over many years. Some have staff who come from the IRLOs and the immigrant and refugee communities they work with. We also build long-term relationships in immigrant and refugee communities by participating in community life and activities, or by advocating on issues that matter to the community.

- *Communication and information sharing.* Transparency and open communication help to build strong, equitable, and trusting relationships. Nexus partners share all reports and documents with IRLOs. We use a variety of methods to clearly communicate expectations (for example, program requirements), or to get clear agreement on shared expectations. Then it is our responsibility to follow through on what we said we'd do, and to help others do the same.

- *Practicing humility.* As capacity builders, we must intentionally demonstrate our vulnerability and willingness to learn and diminish the power differential our role can create. Meeting in the IRLO's "power space" is one way to do that. Nexus partners know it is important to listen a lot and to listen well. We try to show respect and to be humble. One way we model reciprocal learning is to ask the question, "What do I need to learn from you to make me more effective in working with you?" Nexus partners also invite critique from others and critique themselves. This creates an environment in which mistakes (ours and theirs) are accepted and used for learning.

- *Valuing and engaging IRLO knowledge, skills, and experience.* For some Nexus partners, this is a fundamental core value that is used to structurally shape programs. Techniques we use include popular education approaches that draw out and validate people's knowledge and experience, participatory processes, and peer learning.

- *Demonstrating integrity.* In order to build trust, we show that we are trustworthy. One of us calls this "consistent action over time," and says "I demonstrate this by showing up, following up, saying what I mean, and meaning what I say." We build trust by being professional, respecting confidentiality, being timely, and being accurate.

- *Providing useful resources and services.* We can also demonstrate our intent and usefulness as an ally. Nexus partners may do this simply by providing useful and effective products and services (for example, a newsletter, membership list, or training), especially if they are free or low cost. We also help make connections and lower barriers to mainstream resources and institutions.

- *Appropriately supporting or challenging norms.* An important role for us in our work with IRLOs is articulating what the implications of various choices are. After we have built a foundation of trust and relationship, we may need to respectfully challenge IRLO practices and norms. In that case, we are thoughtful and intentional about 1) observing what norms might need to be challenged (such as how elders perceive a younger generation) and 2) thinking about *who* should push those conversations.

This list has just skimmed the surface. Other practitioners will find different ways of addressing these effectiveness factors, and each of us will find different ways of implementing these practices in our own capacity building work.

CHAPTER TWO

SHARED JOURNEYS IN PRACTICE

Each Nexus partner chose a practice that contributes to their effectiveness with IRLOs to share in the form of a case study.

These practices we consider tried and true, and either a cornerstone of our work or a contributor to multiple effectiveness factors. We hope that our stories and practices will prove useful to other capacity builders.

The case studies all follow the same format. First, we provide necessary background on the Nexus partner and the particular organization the partner profiled. (Note that in many cases, the name of the profiled organization was changed to protect its confidentiality.) Next, a practice is described by highlighting how the Nexus partner applied the practice when working with the specific organization they profiled. Finally, a brief analysis highlights the factors or underlying principles that the contributing Nexus partner believes make the practice successful. It is these factors that we hope others will learn from, as they can be translated for application with other practices and other types of organizations.

Participatory Learning and Constituency Leadership Development

Ann Philbin and Luz Rodriguez

Background

The Center to Support Immigrant Organizing (CSIO) works with immigrant organizers, groups, organizations, and collaboratives to help strengthen immigrant community capacity to organize for social, economic, and political justice. The approach to organizing that we promote is grassroots organizing based on *constituency leadership development*. For CSIO, *constituency leadership* means that members of the population an organization represents, organizes, or serves are in decision-making positions within that organization, serving as board, staff, volunteers, and members. The voice of the constituency is the driving force. It determines the direction of the organization and its programs, campaigns, and services. CSIO promotes constituency leadership development in all of its activities.

We believe that the core of the leadership development experience for immigrants in the United States is having the opportunity to use one's skills, experiences, and knowledge to work on behalf of the community. This allows people to unlock their potential; feel the value of their skills, history, and experience; and contribute these toward the common good of their communities. The leadership development process should be a participatory process that helps people move from a position in which they feel powerless or acted upon to one in which they feel able to effect change in the circumstances of their life. CSIO works with immigrant organizations and leaders to help create a continuum of change, moving from the personal level to collective action for societal change.

The Organizers of Color Initiative (OCI) was launched in February 2004 as an effort to support the recruitment and retention of organizers of color in the greater Boston area. CSIO worked with participants to design eight peer-learning sessions. The main purpose of the sessions was to help build the group's knowledge about and ability to carry out effective organizing in communities of color. Although attendance at each session varied somewhat, a core of twenty-five to thirty regular participants attended the sessions, representing most of the immigrant and African American communities in the greater Boston area. The sessions touched on topics that the group had selected as primary for their learning, including what organizing is, the role of the organizer, models of organizing, popular education, multicultural organizing, and power analysis.

In early 2004, Norma Martinez, a Salvadoran woman working as a parent organizer in a Boston neighborhood with a large concentration of Central American immigrants, joined the OCI. She had been hired just weeks before in her first paid organizing job. Norma is a very humble person. She entered the OCI without a specific understanding of the skills she had and the skills that a good organizer needs. Slowly, through the course of her participation in the discussions and activities of OCI, she began to realize that what she had been doing was organizing and that, in fact, she was doing it well. She began to see that what was a natural, instinctive process for her was something that others had to work hard to learn.

As Norma became more confident about her work, she began to share more in the group. Others saw her as someone who was doing what they only understood on a theoretical level. They asked her to share her experience—how she was working with people on the ground. She had the opportunity to see and hear that what she was doing was important, that what she was offering to the community had value.

In addition, as Norma developed greater understanding of her practice and greater confidence in her skills, she began to more actively put into practice what she was learning at meetings—putting parents in positions of leadership by helping them talk directly to principals and to the community at large. She implemented a leadership development approach with greater confidence about its central importance to community organizing work.

This knowledge and confidence enabled Norma to go back to her organization and advocate for what she was doing, challenging the executive director, who didn't really understand organizing. She explained that the parents who were coming to the organization were part of the result of her work. Within her organization, she helped to build a sense of accountability to the community and the needs that they were articulating. In addition, the success of her efforts attracted the attention of funders, who began to show greater interest in the organizing work and lend resources to help keep it going.

The impact of Norma's participation in the OCI has been at the personal, group, organizational, and community levels. She has been an inspiration to other participants in the OCI.

Description of the practice

The Center to Support Immigrant Organizing works to create safety, build trust and relationships, and make evident that the leadership, knowledge, and experience of the group are primary to the learning process. Some of the methodologies we use are

- *Participatory planning.* The design of the OCI was an outgrowth of months of dialogue with immigrant and African American organizers. This process helped us to build ownership of the initiative among its constituents before it started.

- *Clear ground rules.* We work with participants to establish ground rules for their communication so that everyone agrees with and reinforces methods of showing respect and building support.

- *Participatory meeting processes.* We go first to participants for answers and draw out what people know in large groups and small groups. We help participants to see that their ideas are influencing the process in the room and forwarding the learning in the group.

- *Discussions of historical context for immigration.* CSIO works to give participants a deeper understanding of the global economic forces that push people here and the role of the U.S. government in creating and sustaining those forces. This context helps to shift the mainstream paradigm about why immigrants are here, and helps overcome the internalized guilt and shame associated with the mainstream stereotypes about immigration.

- *Creating a level playing field.* We work to "level the playing field" in the room and place people equally regardless of their background, culture, race, language, class, status, level of "formal" education, etc.

- *Continuous feedback.* We build ongoing feedback into the design and implementation of sessions. We get feedback from the whole group in each session, work with the OCI participant advisory group to propose agendas and circulate them to participants for input, and reorganize plans when the group indicates that it is necessary.

- *Use a facilitator with deep understanding of the participants.* Our colleague, Luz, is the primary facilitator and coordinator. Luz shares a background similar to the immigrants whom participants are organizing. It is important that she has a position of leadership in the OCI and is modeling a partnership based on facilitative leadership.

Analysis

The stories of other OCI participants are many and varied. The organizers who have participated regularly in the OCI have created a space that has become an important resource for organizers of color in the greater Boston area. The existence of a safe, supportive, trusting, and respectful learning space is an important support for organizers of color, and it has helped to build solidarity across racial, cultural, class, education, immigration status-based, and other differences. We draw the following conclusions from this work:

- *The participatory process is important with IRLOs.* While the impact of the participatory process shared here is *not* exclusive to immigrant communities, it is particularly important in these communities given the barriers immigrants face in U.S. society. Partnership-based, facilitative group processes are central strategies for grounding capacity building work in the experiences of participants, honoring their skills and experiences, and adapting to the limitations of capacity builders who do not share the culture and experiences of the community they are supporting.

- *Leadership development is critical.* Even work that is technical assistance oriented and shorter term in nature should be founded on processes that promote and build constituency leadership.

- *The work requires humility and an assets-based approach.* This work requires the capacity builder to be a humble and deep listener—to believe in people's ability to solve their own problems, to view himself or herself as a co-learner at all times, to step out of the "expert" role and let people show what they can do.

Community
Consulting
Group

The Importance of Context

Emil Angelica and Monica Herrera

Background

In the mid-1980s, a large number of Southeast Asian refugees began arriving in the Twin Cities area and numerous Mutual Assistance Associations (MAAs) were created. Amherst H. Wilder Foundation's Center for Communities (a portion of which is now Community Consulting Group, LLC) created and managed the technical assistance component of a three-year project called the Bicultural Training Partnership to increase the organization capacity of MAAs.

Description of the practice

While many helpful processes evolved from this project, we will focus on a particular training component that helps MAAs manage more effectively. Conversations with IRLO leaders revealed that some incorrectly felt government and funders had singled out their organizations to comply with regulations that were arbitrary. They felt these regulations focused only on IRLOs. In reality, the regulations were not arbitrary; they were basic nonprofit statutes and regulation. The MAAs were not being singled out in this regard.

Attempts to explain nonprofit statutes and regulations did not resolve the leaders' concerns because the explanations assumed an understanding of American culture that they lacked. In particular, these leaders did not have a context for the fit between nonprofits, government, and business. To broadly address this problem, we created a training unit on the historical occurrences and movements that led to the creation of nonprofits and their regulation. The educational environment helped immigrants and refugees feel comfortable asking questions about overall expectations for nonprofit organizations. It also helped them question their organizations' practices and discuss challenges and improvements.

The curriculum is delivered through a workshop that focuses on the historical development of the nonprofit sector in the United States, with special attention to how nonprofits have functioned through the different social change movements in the United States. The workshop is tailored to fit the audience, but the general template covers

- The history of "waves" of immigration (including refugees) in the United States, from the 1840s to the present. Significant contributions of specific groups are incorporated, tailored for the audience attending the workshop.

- Comparison of the government, for-profit, and nonprofit sectors and how they approach purpose, product, staff, finances, and decision making

- Types of nonprofits and how they address different community issues.

- Current issues nonprofits face.

The historical events are captured on a timeline that can be adjusted to fit the experiences of the group attending the workshop. For instance, when the Southeast Asian community attends the workshop, the timeline shows the Vietnam War years, the U.S. social movements at that time (anti-war, civil rights, women's rights, and other movements), and the impact those movements had in expanding the belief that individuals can come together, organize, influence people's lives, and alter public policy. Because the timeline is visual, participants for whom English is a second language can see the development of the nonprofit sector writ large.

We also personalize the history by having participants develop a group timeline of where they were when all the historical events were happening in the United States. This allows participants to discuss U.S. refugee policies and how those policies impact their families and community.

The workshop provides context for many of the roles, responsibilities, and "rules" nonprofits live by. Without this context, the legal and financial obligations of nonprofits sound petty or arbitrary. Hence the participants' pre-workshop impression that the regulations are unfairly applied only to them can be dispelled as they come to understand the reasons for the rules and regulations.

Further, the historical perspective on the development of the discrete roles played by nonprofit, government, and business safely opens the door to discussions of organizational challenges and of the methods or governance models the group can incorporate into their organization.

This practice can be varied based on the meeting time available and the capacity building outcomes desired. For example, the tool can be effective as a warm-up to discussions or as the main way for discussions to take place. In a short meeting, less time can be spent exploring what else was going on in other parts of the world, while if there is more time discussions of worldwide events can actually become the primary way to examine an issue, since it provides other cultural perspectives (including those not represented in the room).

There are several ways that this tool can be applied to work with IRLOs:

- *To facilitate an objective discussion of the questions participants have about nonprofits.* As participants learn about all the components of nonprofit organizations, they can also engage in a cursory assessment of their organization. Invariably, the practice surfaces discussion of what is working well and what is missing or needs to be addressed.

- *To demonstrate how the system has changed over time and will continue to change.* This can be done by reflecting on how and when the changes occurred and what was behind those changes. In some instances it is important to identify the role the IRLO group had in having an impact on the change.

- *To give people a timeline to indicate when they arrived and what changes they have experienced as an organization and as a community.* By using a visual timeline (stretched out on butcher paper on the wall) to highlight the key components of the curriculum, participants see themselves on the timeline and write in changes they experienced. This helps them develop a context for other activities.

- *To explain the change in the United States and put it in the context of what was going on worldwide and in their country of origin.* This approach enables people to use this curriculum as a starting point for discussing what they know about the world and highlighting differences as well as similarities. This process, in turn, helps participants better understand the system in which they are operating.

Analysis

The following principles can be extracted from this practice:

- *Creating a shared cultural context can generate mutual understanding and facilitate shared experiences and learning.*

- *Setting a personal context for U.S. rules and regulations helps immigrants and refugees gain a perspective on social structures in this country.*

- *The creation of a historical and cultural context creates a safe zone for discussing difficult issues.* In this safe zone, the organization's problems are depersonalized. People can see how other individuals and organizations have handled similar problems, used similar strategies, and made similar mistakes. This context helps save face for all participants.

- *A visual, participatory model speeds understanding, especially when English is a second language.* The large graphic timeline also makes it easy for people to revisit the timeline at a later time to deepen understanding and discussion.

COMPASSPOINT NONPROFIT SERVICES

Establishing Rapport

Anushka Fernandopulle and Alfredo Vergara-Lobo

Background

An IRLO called LatinoOut[10] was a neighborhood-based community organization serving a Latino lesbian, gay, bisexual, and transgender (LGBT) community within a particular geographic area. The organization functioned as a community center and a catalyst for various kinds of organizing in the community by providing a space for artistic activity, health education, a celebration of cultural events, and an informal connection. The executive director and most staff and board members came from the organization's client population, and there had been some fluidity among these three groups over the organization's life.

While the CompassPoint consultant assigned to the project was not a member of this community, the consultant did share some experiences through being a member of the LGBT community, an immigrant, and a person of color. The consultant was familiar with some of the history of the Latino LGBT community in the area, knew people who were connected to the organization, and had also participated in some of the larger community festivals and events that LatinoOut had been a part of. The credibility of CompassPoint was also helpful, since it has a reputation among this IRLO's peer organizations as being staffed by and friendly to LGBT groups and communities of color.

Description of the practice

Although there had been opportunities and attempts in the past to hire technical assistance, these had never worked out. The differing accounts of these episodes were telling. From the consultants' accounts, they had held one meeting with the organization, but then nothing had come of it. From the perspective of those in the organization, someone who was not from their community, who they had never seen before, dropped by their office once, spoke in lingo about things that were not so clear, and then never showed up again.

Having discovered this history of failed consulting relationships, the CompassPoint consultant was intentional about connecting with people in the organization and making explicit the shared values and experiences that they had. The consultant invested time in attending community events and

---

[10] Fictional name

getting to know the organization. At the same time the consultant was also clear about what their differences were in identity and community and tried to acknowledge and bridge these as well.

The consultant was also clear about discussing up front some of the expectations and concerns around communication in the project. For example, the project was funded by a third party, meaning that it appeared to the client organization as "free" in terms of money. We highlighted the time expenditure that was going to be involved for the client as part of their investment. We also talked about communication with the third-party funder and what would and would not be reported to them. For example, we would share the general work plan for the project with the funder, but we would not share the organizational assessment that would emerge during the engagement and inform the work plan. This allowed the client organization to feel more willing to fully share what was going on in their situation. Such disclosure would be essential to our ability to create a capacity building plan that addressed their true needs.

This particular capacity building engagement lasted for a year. One of the activities we did early on in our time together was to hold a one-day training for board members with the goal of increasing the board's effectiveness as a group. While we had prepared for the session with the executive director and board leadership, it quickly became clear that many of the attendees were not very engaged in the session. We chose to interrupt the flow of the agenda and ask them why. After some discussion, it surfaced that many people wanted a very different way of accomplishing the end goal. We quickly adapted our practices to make the training more of a coaching and mentoring session. Most importantly, through this intervention we made sure that the clients understood that they were in control of the choice of what content they needed and how they should best receive it.

Our work continued together over the year and by all accounts enabled the organization to work more effectively together and accomplish their mission with greater success. After our engagement, the organization also developed further skills in working with outside consultants and engaged several others to do other kinds of work with them in the following years.

Analysis

- *Understanding the dynamics of trust and relationships for immigrant and refugee (and in this case LGBT) communities was a major success factor.* We understand that many immigrant and refugee people have had negative experiences in purely transactional relationships in the marketplace. People who are perceived as immigrants—especially people of color and those who are perceived as non-native English speakers—are not always treated well or with respect (or given a good deal) in such transactions. Many immigrants and refugees prefer to deal with someone they know within their community for services when possible; for example, going to someone in the community who can fix cars rather than going to a general auto shop (that may even be closer).

- *Building a relationship of trust is key in providing service to immigrant and refugee groups.* In this engagement it was very helpful for the consultant to have shared experience as an immigrant, some shared community connections in a broader LGBT community, and further to actively spend time cultivating relationships with people in the organization and community. It was also helpful to make explicit the shared values we had around social justice and a recognition of dynamics of oppression. Thus connecting on shared characteristics but understanding the dynamics of difference contributed to our success together.

- *CompassPoint's model for process consulting (as taught in our Institute for Nonprofit Consulting) was also helpful in this engagement.* The model helped us focus on being client-centered and on adapting to their needs, mode of learning, and communication style, as evidenced in the story about the board retreat. The group conversation we had in the middle of the retreat allowed the client to use the consultant at their discretion and empowered the client to choose the way content was delivered.

TWIN CITIES LOCAL INITIATIVES SUPPORT CORPORATION (LISC)

Funder as Ally

Barb Jeanetta

Background

Local Initiatives Support Corporation (LISC) provides financial and technical assistance to community-based organizations engaged in practices that improve the livability and economy of their communities—especially for those most marginalized from mainstream economy and policies. We have made an intentional effort over the past several years to build more relationships with IRLOs and other communities of color to better understand their housing interests and needs and help them realize their community development dreams.

In late 2003, LISC issued a request for proposal to IRLOs and organizations in communities of color that had an interest in building their capacity to develop affordable housing. Leading up to that request, LISC contacted many of its IRLO connections to discuss the proposal, their interest in applying for it, and various strategies and options for approaching the work.

LISC was able to commit operating dollars and more intensive technical assistance to four organizations over a two-year period. These organizations had all demonstrated some degree of readiness by articulating a housing project that aligned with their communities' needs, by proposing a capacity building plan to accomplish the project, and by providing a draft budget.

One of these four organizations is a social service organization that is based in and led by Southeast Asians. The group, which we'll call SER,[11] wanted to develop homes that were designed to suit the larger family sizes and cultural practices of the Hmong community. SER had been in operation for twenty years and was widely recognized for its creativity in improving the lives of Southeast Asian families. However, it had never engaged in any real estate development and had always leased office space.

As noted previously, several conversations preceded SER's formal proposal for LISC funding. We discussed various alternative approaches to accomplishing a real estate development project and the implications of each for SER. SER decided to hire a part-time staff person (the "housing project

---

[11] Fictional name

manager") to focus on housing issues and to partner with a more experienced nonprofit developer until it was able to manage the process on its own. LISC committed two years of operating support, management assistance, and more intensive technical assistance from LISC staff beginning in the winter of 2004.

The LISC liaison meets with SER's executive director and housing project manager periodically to check on progress against their goals and next steps. LISC views its role as an advocate or ally for SER as it works to achieve its plan. Acting in this role, the LISC liaison has suggested and provided reference to other funding sources and has helped SER explore options to refine or adjust its approach and timeline. For example, SER went through an executive director transition midway through the first year grant. Most of SER's progress on the housing project stopped during the transition. LISC was patient. After consulting the board, the new director decided to modify the housing development goal to better serve the organization's core constituency. He thought a rental housing project made more sense given many of their constituents' income. LISC was amenable to the change and has adjusted the work plan and timeline accordingly.

The LISC liaison provides a modest amount of technical assistance. The liaison's focus is helping SER understand the real estate development process, potential financing sources, and other potential resources (training, expertise, comparable projects). The LISC liaison has also helped SER understand the implications of real estate development and management for their organization and its governance process. Usually, this technical assistance is provided "just in time" or as issues arise. It is done as an ally, or as a person with the best interests of their organization in mind (rather than as oversight or grant monitoring).

The grant dollars will continue through the end of 2006. LISC's relationship with SER will continue beyond that if the organization has not yet completed its housing development goals or decides to expand them.

Description of the practice

- Match resources to organizational and community interests—determine who is interested in affordable housing development and send them a request for proposal.

- Work with organizations to explore strategies *before* proposal submission and help them frame their proposal.

- Build working relationships with key staff of organizations—listen as an ally, offer suggestions or alternatives and discuss related implications, and trust them to choose the best strategies for the organization.

- Provide operating support, coupled with assistance in identifying and acquiring appropriate technical assistance and training, on the IRLO's time frame. This is a resource that wouldn't normally be available for a new entrant into the housing development field.

- Meet periodically, at their office, to discuss progress and refine the approach or timeline.

Analysis

- *Operating dollars to support the organization are key to being able to effectively build internal capacity.* There is a cost to spending adequate time on new project development. While technical assistance and advice are important, they don't cover operating costs.

- *Building a trusting relationship is important.* The organization needs to view LISC as an ally and advocate for their success (rather than as funder and monitor) and trust that positive criticism or correction is offered in their interest. This means the LISC liaison needs to be clear about his or her role, expectations for the grantee, and in what case or instances LISC funding would be withdrawn or changed.

- *Organizations need assistance in considering various approaches to building real estate development capacity and completing project goals.* This avoids their having to "reinvent the wheel," bumbling through, or bringing unnecessary risk to their organization. They are in the best position to judge what approach will work best in their organizational culture and structure.

- *It is not likely that the original plan and timeline will proceed without adjustment or refinement.* A funder or technical assistance provider's flexibility on these matters is key.

- *It is challenging to a) help the organization maintain a community voice in their housing plans and projects and b) build institutional skills and infrastructure (such as strategic plans, organizational culture, and board training) that can be maintained beyond any one staff person.*

MAP FOR NONPROFITS

Opening the Door

Charley Ravine

Background

MAP for Nonprofits is a management support organization providing a comprehensive range of services and technical assistance for nonprofit organizations in Minnesota. MAP for Nonprofits has over twenty-five years of experience working with nonprofits, including many immigrant- and refugee-led organizations. Among these services is legal assistance for nonprofits, either via direct help with issues such as filing papers or mergers, or via a "hotline" subscription service that provides answers to questions the nonprofit may have. Often, a new organization's first contact with capacity building services happens when they approach MAP for help in forming a nonprofit corporation. By providing accessible, high-quality services at this entry point, MAP builds trust and opens the door to a long-term capacity building relationship as the organization's needs evolve.

The African Leadership Group (ALG)[12] is an IRLO organized to provide leadership training to African immigrant organizations, utilizing African cultural values, perceptions, and context for learning. ALG also serves as a bridge to help funders, mainstream organizations, and agencies understand the barriers and difficulties immigrant and refugee leaders encounter in running their organizations.

Description of the practice

Asiya Mohamed,[13] a Somalian leader, founded ALG in 2000. She came to MAP for Nonprofits initially for assistance to incorporate and to complete the Application for Recognition of 501(c)(3) status from the IRS. She came to MAP because of its reputation for affordable, accessible, and effective legal services for nonprofit organizations. Asiya met with MAP's staff attorney, who had worked with hundreds of nonprofits on these issues. The vast majority of those organizations in recent years had been IRLOs. Asiya, typical of those who come to MAP for incorporation, had little experience with the U.S. legal system or with U.S. nonprofits.

After an initial conversation, the staff attorney reviewed and explained the various forms and documents necessary to the whole process, and began to collect information needed to draft documents and complete paperwork.

---

[12] Fictional name
[13] Fictional name

Asiya left the meeting with assignments to gather information and make decisions on what had been discussed. One key part of the application process to the IRS is developing a three-year budget and detailed written description of their programs, services, and activities. The attorney provided a format and guidance for each. There were many e-mails and a few phone calls and meetings over the next few months, as ALG's plan and projected budget were developed. Because of language difficulty and inexperience with the American legal system, Asiya relied heavily on the attorney to guide and educate her about the process, and what it means to form a nonprofit in the United States. But most of the questions in the process were ones that Asiya had to answer, based on ALG's own goals and preferences.

The process was completed in late 2001, allowing ALG to start operations at a minimum level. Even before the IRS application was approved, Asiya was talking with other MAP staff about board training. In 2004, ALG subscribed to MAP's Legal Hot Line, which provides ongoing access to legal assistance (renewable annually), and remains a subscriber to this day. ALG also contracted with MAP for accounting services and had MAP prepare its 990 for 2004. Finally, the organization contracted with MAP for technology planning and implementation, which was completed in May 2005. The accounting consultant found that with time he was able to develop a communication style that allowed him to better assist Asiya in understanding accounting concepts. The trust that developed led to open communication about programs, which in turn informed the consultant, enabling him to develop an accounting system which met the needs of the organization. This ultimately made it easier for the Asiya to present financial reports to the board of directors. With MAP's assistance, ALG grew from a $17,000 budget in 2001 to $160,000 in 2004.

Analysis

- *Welcoming is important at the first point of contact.* Legal services are often the initial entry into MAP for IRLOs. It is not unusual for these clients to show up without an appointment, and the attorney will meet with them if he is able, even when it means interrupting other work. The attorney will also schedule meetings quickly—typically within a few days.

- *Work to build trust.* Providing quality services to IRLOs over time has given MAP a positive reputation in immigrant and refugee communities; most organizations now come to MAP based on referrals from people they know. Trust builds gradually as MAP works with the organization. The staff attorney's extensive experience helps ensure reliable quality of service.

- *Cost accessibility helps open the door.* MAP provides free initial conversations in each of its service areas, and its services are inexpensive compared with those of other providers. MAP currently has a scholarship fund that can pay or partially cover fees. Organizations may also be referred to a nonprofit assistance fund.

- *Connecting to multiple services can broaden the relationship.* Early on, the attorney gives the client a list of services MAP can provide. Over time, he will connect them with people or services more directly, as opportunities arise. Often, he will introduce them personally to the appropriate MAP consultant. The diversity of MAP's staff (it's "bench strength") facilitates these connections.

NONPROFIT ASSISTANCE CENTER

**NONPROFIT
ASSISTANCE
CENTER**

Intensive Technical Assistance

Vicki Asakura and Barbara Fane

Background

The Nonprofit Assistance Center (NAC) is a social change organization with a mission to empower communities by building strong nonprofits and community leaders and to shape institutions and policy to achieve social justice and equity. We influence and guide the practice of the nonprofit sector and other institutions through technical assistance, training, leadership development, and community-based research and evaluation. NAC provides direct technical assistance to organizations without charge, and also acts as an intermediary, awarding funds that organizations use to pay for capacity building services. We prioritize our services to communities of color, those with low income, refugees and immigrants, and other groups that currently or historically faced discrimination and have little access to resources. NAC also works with the broader nonprofit sector and other institutions to affect system-level change toward achieving equity.

The focus of this case study is SeaRef,[14] which is led by and serves refugee women in the greater Seattle-King County area of Washington State. NAC has had a rich, twenty-five-year history with this organization.

SeaRef is a multi-ethnic organization, providing culturally and linguistically appropriate services to refugee and immigrant women and their families, while advocating for social justice, public policy changes, and equal access to services. This organization has grown tremendously in the past several years and is in major transition. SeaRef's management staff now has responsibilities spread over several locations and program areas.

The relationship is highly valued by both NAC and the SeaRef. When the organization had technical assistance needs, it felt NAC was readily accessible and approached NAC to discuss capacity building. NAC staff was deliberate in listening to what the organization was saying about its current organizational development situation. Staff from the two organizations met several times prior to discuss challenges and options. The informal meetings helped to strengthen the relationship and ensured that each partner was truly hearing what the other was saying. After discussions, SeaRef formally applied to NAC for service. SeaRef was awarded

---

[14] Fictional name

technical assistance funds to pay for consultant services to codesign and facilitate a project to 1) improve teamwork; 2) strengthen communication; and 3) develop leadership skills and provide mentoring and coaching for the executive director.

NAC then conducted an interactive assessment with the executive director. SeaRef drove the work plan by selecting and prioritizing work areas based on information from the assessment. Together, NAC and SeaRef developed a customized work plan, allocating adequate resources, especially time, for the project to be completed. The organization was also offered different technical assistance options, allowing the executive director to determine the type and content of capacity building, as well as which consultant to engage to help implement the plan. SeaRef chose a consultant from NAC's extensive local referral network. The details regarding the relationship between the executive director and the consultant of choice were kept confidential and unavailable to NAC, although NAC maintained frequent and open communication with both the client and the consultant. Evaluation results showed that the organization achieved broad buy-in for organizational change and that managers felt empowered to set goals and take action to build the team and enhance communication.

Description of the practice

This successful capacity building engagement relied on four key factors: engagement, empowerment, support, and evaluation.

- *Engagement:* The first key is mutual respect and trust as a basis for the IRLO accessing technical assistance and partnering with NAC. This particular relationship was built over several years, but even shorter relationships can be fruitful if they are built on respect, trust, and shared values.

- *Empowerment:* The client organization drove the process through a simple, interactive assessment process, selecting priorities, developing the work plan, and contracting with the consultant directly.

- *Support:* NAC provided referrals, served as a liaison, and respected confidentiality between the IRLO and consultant. NAC maintains a pool of referral consultants with both technical expertise and cultural competence that organizations may use to identify consultants they hire.

- *Evaluation:* NAC's technical assistance also included funding for follow-up capacity building and evaluation.

Analysis

The intensive technical assistance approach works both with IRLOs and other types of nonprofits. The basic philosophy is asset based: organizations already have many of the assets and some of the resources they need to create solutions with support from technical assistance providers.

There are many strengths to this intensive approach:

- *The practitioner develops relationships that present further opportunities.* The relationships open the door to future networking and collaborating, and bring in knowledge about the organization and community.

- *The approach is respectful.* It values the organization or community and allows the client organization's voice to be heard.

- *The client organization is empowered.* It is supported to take responsibility for solving the issues the organization and community face.

- *The practitioner is a partner rather than a "rescuing" expert.* Thus, organizations value the time the practitioner invests in them professionally and personally.

- *The provision of funding for technical assistance affords the client the capacity to address issues.*

- *The practice has inherent values of cultural competency, flexibility, and adaptability.* It can be used to respond to emergent issues facing IRLOs. The holistic approach to organizational development builds the capacity in foundational areas, which will promote sustainability.

There are some weaknesses to the use of this approach as well. First, this practice requires a large investment of time during and outside of the normal workday, beginning before there is a formal application for service. Second, this practice is more costly that other practices in time, dollars, and human resources.

This practice works most effectively with a comprehensive approach over long-term engagement and is less suited to individual, one-of-a-kind services.

Leveraged Capacity Building

MO✴SAICA

Hilary Binder-Aviles

Background

Mosaica works in partnership with national IRLOs to provide capacity building assistance to community-based (or "local") IRLOs affiliated with the national IRLO. This case study is based on a composite of several different capacity building initiatives that were funded through three-year federal grants. The composite national IRLO profiled in this case study, which we'll call the National Refugee Network,[15] serves as an "umbrella" organization for a network of local, community-based IRLOs that serve the same refugee community. The National Refugee Network exists to strengthen the local IRLOs, to convene local IRLO leaders to learn from each other, and to advocate for refugees at a national level. The National Refugee Network contracted with Mosaica to provide training and technical assistance designed to strengthen the local IRLOs, with a focus on board development, resource development, financial management, program planning, management, evaluation, collaboration, and coalition building. The initiative included a series of one- to three-day regional training seminars for local IRLOs, as well as targeted assistance to individual local IRLOs. The federal grant that supported this capacity building initiative also provided subgrants to the local IRLOs.

Description of the practice

Designing the training: Mosaica and the National Refugee Network sat down as partners and discussed the objectives of the training. The National Refugee Network shared its perspectives on the local IRLOs' strengths, areas for improvements, needs, challenges, and issues of concern.

Conducting training: Mosaica was the lead facilitator and trainer, while the staff of the National Refugee Network played a key role in observing, listening, and adding and clarifying issues throughout the training session, often challenging the local IRLOs to address tough issues.

Developing technical assistance plans: Mosaica provided training to National Refugee Network staff on how to conduct organizational assessments and develop technical assistance plans. National Refugee Network staff, as part of regular site visits to the local IRLOs that are part of its network, then

---

[15] Fictional name

conducted assessments and worked with the local IRLOs to identify objectives for technical assistance (such as getting the board more active, diversifying funding, or creating systems for planning and evaluation).

Providing on-site technical assistance: One or two Mosaica staff and one or two staff from the National Refugee Network provided on-site technical assistance as a team. This assistance ranged from facilitating board planning sessions and reviewing financial management systems, to assistance in designing new programs and developing proposals for funders.

Follow-up technical assistance: The staff of the National Refugee Network then took the lead on any follow-up with the local IRLOs. This included sending out the training and meeting notes that Mosaica prepared, following up on next steps, and making check-in calls, with Mosaica playing a supportive role to IRLO staff (for example, the IRLO staff contacted Mosaica directly for advice or materials).

Analysis

Mosaica's experience with the National Refugee Network suggests the following principles for working in partnership with other IRLOs:

- *Capitalize on the complementary strengths of the partnering organizations.* In this case, Mosaica brought its technical expertise in organizational development and the National Refugee Network brought its knowledge of the specific refugee and immigrant community (its language, culture, history, and experiences in the United States) along with an existing relationship with and knowledge of the local IRLO (its history, reputation, strengths, challenges, leaders, and so forth). In planning the training, we identified topics that should be led by the National Refugee Network because of their expertise. For example, in a training seminar about managing conflict, Mosaica facilitated the overall training while the National Refugee Network led the discussion about traditional methods for managing conflict from the IRLO's home country.

- *Use the partnership to ensure that training topics and methodologies are relevant and tailored to the specific ethnic community.* By designing the training in consultation with the National Refugee Network, we ensured that all of the training activities—such as small group discussion questions and problem-solving scenarios—reflected the actual issues the local IRLOs are facing and took into account the cultural and community context of their work.

- *Take advantage of the shared learning opportunities offered by partnership.* Our approach does not assume that any single partner—the consultant, the National Refugee Network, or the local IRLO—has all the answers. Each partner offered different experience and expertise, and we learned from each other. For example, while the IRLOs learned from Mosaica about the expectations of a nonprofit board in the United States, Mosaica learned about issues related to building trust with communities, a particular concern for the boards of the local IRLOs.

- *Partnership facilitates the creation of organizational best practices for local IRLOs.* By creating the space for mutual learning, we were able to identify new "best organizational development practices" drawn directly from the IRLOs' experiences. For example, in a series of training seminars on collaboration, Mosaica provided an overall framework for understanding how collaboration works, while the IRLOs shared their challenges in collaborating with non-IRLOs. Together, we analyzed their experience, teased out lessons learned, and developed tools (for example, checklists of questions to ask a potential partner) designed to support IRLOs in collaborating with non-IRLOs.

- *Find ways to establish a base of trust and credibility.* Mosaica's relationship with the National Refugee Network and the local IRLOs helped this process. Because we came to the training or a local IRLO site with the umbrella National Refugee Network, which already had a relationship with the local IRLO, there was already a basic level of trust with the local groups.

- *Leverage partnerships to build network capacity.* The partnership between Mosaica and the National Refugee Network strengthened the relationship between the National Refugee Network and its community-based partners. With the National Refugee Network playing a key role in the training and technical assistance, our approach helps to increase the visibility and credibility of the National Refugee Network with its network.

Critical to making this approach work is the trust and mutual respect between Mosaica and the National Refugee Network. We have a long-term relationship and shared commitment to strengthening community-based, immigrant- and refugee-led organizations and the communities they serve. We have also found that it is important to agree on roles and responsibilities in both the training and technical assistance components, and to have regular and open communication.

PARTNERSHIP FOR IMMIGRANT LEADERSHIP AND ACTION

Partnership for Immigrant
Leadership and Action

From Vision to Planning

Heba Nimr and Monica Regan

Background

Partnership for Immigrant Leadership and Action (PILA) works to increase civic and political activism among low-income immigrant communities to strengthen democracy and advance social justice. PILA designs and leads innovative capacity building programs that support grassroots leadership development, voter education, and other strategies for strengthening immigrant political power and participation.

PILA's core program strategy is to support Northern California organizations based in immigrant communities by intentionally incorporating leadership development of their constituents into their ongoing programs and services. Toward this goal, PILA conducts intensive, year-long multilingual leadership programs, bringing together a diverse group of partner organizations. Early in the program, partner organizations develop work plans to guide their efforts to build immigrant leadership in their communities. They then implement the work plan throughout the remaining duration of the program.

The process of creating a work plan is a fundamental practice in PILA's programs. Through it, partner organizations articulate leadership development goals particular to their organizations' work and context. They map the activities they anticipate will realize those goals, who is responsible for the activities, and a projected timeline. In addition, partner organizations identify outcomes by which they will measure their progress toward meeting their goals. The work planning and implementation process is interwoven throughout and complemented by the other components of the intensive program—including training, technical assistance, coaching, and opportunities for peer learning and reflection in one-on-one as well as group formats.

One particular organization's experience is a good illustration of the role and importance of work planning in PILA's capacity building efforts. Mission Housing Support (MHS)[16] is a seven-staff, membership organization that provides advice and services to low-income, primarily Latino immigrant tenants concentrated in two San Francisco neighborhoods. During PILA's needs assessment process, MHS articulated a strong organizational value of supporting constituency leadership development toward collective

---

[16] Fictional name

community action. MHS, however, had few systematic strategies to incorporate the value into its services and programs. In addition, MHS noted that while every staff member felt that leadership development of community members was some part of his or her job, none of them was sure of his or her specific role in the process.

Description of the practice

Two MHS staff and three community members participated in PILA's year-long program, joining forty staff and community participants from fourteen other diverse organizations. Participants engaged in relationship building and interactive exercises with their peers. These efforts supported the development of a collective long-term vision for social change that all participant organizations would work toward. The exercises increased their understanding of the value of grassroots leadership development in bringing about that vision. MHS and each of the other individual organizations then articulated their own shorter-term vision of what would look different in each of their communities if their leadership development and community action efforts were successful.

In a subsequent, focused session, PILA introduced a framework for organizations to translate their vision into an action plan by identifying specific leadership development goals, strategies, and outcomes. With their peers in the training setting, MHS participants began brainstorming their goals for the year.

Back at MHS, over the course of several weeks, MHS participants worked with a team of staff and community members to more specifically brainstorm the elements of their work plan, which they submitted in draft form to PILA. The specific areas they chose to focus on were 1) formalizing a community education leadership institute to expand their membership and base of core community leaders; 2) connecting their community education efforts to both identify and act on a larger community action project; and 3) incorporating constituency leadership development into their organizational structure more systemically.

PILA then did a site visit to MHS and worked with the team to flesh out key strategies and engage in a general "reality-check" discussion on the specifics of their plan. Like other organizations at this stage, MHS's goals were ambitious. After the site visit, the MHS team finalized its work plan in a format that was understandable and usable by MHS's staff and community participants.

MHS began implementing its plan in its community. Concurrently, MHS staff and members continued to participate in PILA's capacity building program, which provided guidance and training on various constituency leadership development strategies, models, and activities that could be used in implementing their plan. During these sessions, MHS participants checked in with their peers on progress toward achieving their goals. With training peers from other organizations, the full MHS staff, and community participants, MHS continued to reflect on and revise its plan throughout the year.

At the end of the program, MHS evaluated its progress toward the constituency leadership development goals set forth in the work plan. They found that they had expanded their membership base from 100 to 150 and had more than doubled their core community leadership to twenty. With training and support provided by MHS, this leadership and membership base had worked with MHS staff to lead an effort to defeat a city ballot initiative that failed to adequately address the need for more affordable housing. Finally, MHS had developed a more systematic member-leadership structure by the end of the year. In their evaluation of PILA's capacity building program, MHS identified the work plan as a critical factor in supporting its accomplishments. The continuous cycle of planning, action, and reflection modeled in the program helped MHS turn a vision for constituency leadership into a concrete reality.

Analysis

Through its partnership with MHS and dozens of other similar organizations, PILA has learned the following about the role of the work planning process in capacity building:

- *The work plan is a critical element in ensuring client-centered practice.* In the context of programs that have multiple participants, the work planning process is necessary to ensure that the program's lessons are relevant to and centered around the specific needs of each organizational participant.

- *Peer learning increases effectiveness.* The work plan's effectiveness as a dynamic learning tool is significantly furthered when organizations share and reflect on their work plans in a peer learning setting.

- *Participatory processes result in improved goal fulfillment.* Goals are more likely to be achieved when the plan development process is participatory, involving all the members of the team that will be charged with its implementation. Involvement from the development stage builds buy-in, just as regular progress check-ins and adjustments to changing circumstances keep the plan alive and useful.

- *The work plan must fit the organization's culture.* It is less important that the work plan conform to a specific style than it is for the plan to make sense and provide a common planning language among those within the organization who implement it, and keep it a living, useful document. By developing their own internal language, organizations can better adapt the planning, reflection, and evaluation practices encouraged by work planning to other organizational development areas.

- *The process of creating a work plan can increase work visibility and communicability.* The work plan process requires an organization to name its vision, attach goals to its vision, act on the goals, reflect on them, and then evaluate its progress. This process makes progress toward outcomes and key accomplishments more visible and thus easier to value and communicate within, as well as outside, an organization.

REFUGEEWORKS

Talking Success

Cheryl Hamilton

Background

As the national center for refugee employment, RefugeeWorks hosts six employment-training institutes each year for the National Refugee Employment network. The objective of the two-day institute is to enhance the skills and knowledge of frontline service providers so they may better assist refugees in their effort to integrate into the American workforce. The trainings draw staff from immigrant- and refugee-serving organizations (such as national voluntary agencies responsible for refugee resettlement, state refugee programs, and local workforce development offices), as well as immigrant- and refugee-led organizations. In 2004, RefugeeWorks hosted a Hmong Employment Training Institute in Fresno, California, following the resettlement of several thousand Hmong refugees across the United States. Staff from several organizations led by Hmong Americans joined voluntary agency and workforce development staff at the training.

RefugeeWorks designs employee training institutes with particular consideration for the unique cultural and capacity needs of IRLO participants. From encouraging peer learning between participants to offering scholarships to IRLOs (in this case Hmong organizations) RefugeeWorks continually strives to strengthen relationships between IRLOs and other providers in the refugee employment network. With stronger relationships, IRLO and their partner agencies are better equipped to overcome refugee employment barriers, such as the particular marketing challenge described in the following practice description.

Description of the practice

The purpose of the Fresno Employment Training Institute was for participants to learn the skills required for helping a newly-arrived refugee secure employment in the United States, with special emphasis on the cultural and historical background of Hmong refugees. Some of the topics covered in the training included marketing, job development, nurturing employer relations, case reporting, and career laddering. Hosted on-site at a local IRLO training facility, RefugeeWorks utilized a variety of hands-on, interactive methods of learning to engage participants, such as role playing, case report analysis, and small group exchange. The curriculum was developed with guidance from the local host to ensure that the training participants gained relevant information and skills to enhance their refugee employment services (such local guidance is customary for us). RefugeeWorks also sought feedback on curriculum development from their advisory board, which includes several IRLO representatives.

Similar to the other employment training institutes hosted in cities across the country, RefugeeWorks began the Fresno training with a two-hour workshop entitled "How We Talk about Refugees." The decision to start with this particular workshop stems from observations of the unique communication challenges employment providers face when talking about refugees, whether speaking to the media or pitching a client to a potential employer. Depending on the words or phrases chosen, providers can create a positive or negative impression of a new refugee population, which can affect an individual's ability to secure work. Throughout the workshop, providers reflect on how their presentation of refugees either creates or breaks down barriers to refugee employment.

The main components of the workshop include a combination of media analysis, critical thinking, role playing, and peer evaluation. In Fresno, the workshop began with participants reading a selection of newspaper articles related to the Hmong resettlement, which included direct quotes from staff at IRLOs and refugee-serving agencies. For example, in one article an executive director of an IRLO is quoted as saying, "I am worried [that] because [Hmong refugees] have low job skills, they will not be able to find employment." In the discussion which followed, providers were asked to share their reactions to the articles and evaluate the impression employers might gain of refugees after reading the material. Inevitably, some providers were disappointed with the description of Hmong refugees, whereas others did not find any problems. The trainers used these points of contention to launch a lengthy discussion on critical thinking and marketing. Participants examined how their own language and stereotypes influence other people's perception of refugees and similarly, IRLOs and other refugee-serving agencies. To improve their marketing approach, participants engaged in a role play following the discussion. A job developer practiced his or her employer pitch with a fellow colleague pretending to be an employer, while the other participants offered constructive feedback to their peers. In the end, many people began to realize the significant role they play in representing refugees in a way that celebrates the skills and assets refugees bring to many employers.

Analysis

The Employment Training Institutes, and more specifically the introductory workshop on critical thinking and communication called "How We Talk about Refugees," incorporate several of the seven successful effectiveness factors, particularly the three related to cultural competency, participatory methods, and peer learning.

- *Cultural competency.* With regards to cultural competency, RefugeeWorks' trainers are honest during workshops about how their identity and dialogue shapes public opinion. By acknowledging the importance of being self-aware, trainers begin to bridge cultural differences between themselves and the participants. For example, none of the trainers at the Fresno Institute were immigrants or of Hmong descent, so it was particularly important for the trainers to ask for feedback from the Hmong American participants on how their presentation of the newly-arrived refugees was interpreted. Also, by gently introducing the topic of cultural competency early on in the two-day training, RefugeeWorks staff established a richer foundation for thoughtful discussion during the more skill-based sessions that followed. Participants gave more critical consideration to the context in which their daily work is conducted than they had in past programs in which this particular workshop was excluded.

- *Participatory methods and peer learning.* In evaluations, IRLO staff and other participants express that they appreciate the trainings because of the networking opportunities that arise from RefugeeWorks' utilization of participatory methods and peer learning. With very few lecture style workshops, the staff from IRLOs continually interact with and learn from partners within the field, while sharing their own skills and assets with others. In Fresno, the providers from Hmong agencies were able to explain cultural behaviors of Hmong refugee clients for non-Hmong participants, while everyone gained new skills in job development.

While the institutes have several strengths, there are also limitations to the model. Because the institute lasts only two days, RefugeeWorks' engagement with the IRLO participants is limited, making the peer relationships fostered even more important. In some situations, RefugeeWorks provides additional training and consultation to specific IRLOs; however, this is often again only on a short-term basis. Additionally, although the institutes are a good introduction to the refugee employment field, IRLOs and other agencies in the refugee employment network could benefit from having other local training options available to them on a regular basis. These trainings would allow participants to reflect on their work, draw from each others' experiences, learn about new trends and provide a forum for local providers to collaboratively improve the employment services that are available to newly-arrived refugees.

UNITED WAY OF GREATER TORONTO

**United Way
of Greater Toronto**

Team Based Capacity Building

Amanuel Melles and Anne Pyke

Background

In 2005, United Way of Greater Toronto (UWGT) provided over $50 million in core and program funding to social service agencies in Toronto. In addition to this key funding, UWGT has also been providing organizational capacity building support to its member agencies for the past fifteen years, including organizational change processes to promote equity and diversity; a volunteer consultant program with individuals who have expertise in strategic planning, governance, and human resources; and currently, a leadership program for middle managers to promote succession planning for diverse ethno-racial groups. Given Toronto's multicultural character, UWGT as a whole has also adopted a priority area to support and promote ethno-racial diversity—Helping Newcomers Fulfill Their Promise and Potential.

One of the capacity building projects within the newcomer priority area is Capacity Building for Community Impact (CBCI). CBCI is a three-year organizational development pilot program to strengthen the capacity of five agencies which serve immigrants and refugees in Toronto suburbs. These suburban areas are home to high concentrations of multi-ethnic newcomers. In this pilot program, UWGT staff engage each organization in a capacity assessment process using an assessment tool designed for smaller organizations working with multi-ethnic populations. The facilitator worked with board and staff to determine areas of strength indicated by the tool and areas the organization wished to develop. Once the agency prioritized the areas it wished to develop, the facilitator matched members of a technical assistance team to the agencies to work on the prioritized areas.

Alpha Family Centre is one of the agencies in the CBCI program. Alpha works with families and children in its community to enhance their potential through English language training, settlement services, food access programs, leadership training, job search supports, translation, and interpretation. The community Alpha serves is highly ethno-racially diverse and includes people from Latin America, the Caribbean, Southeast Asia, Africa, and South Asia.

Alpha's organizational assessment indicated a number of areas in which their capacity could be strengthened, including partnership development and visioning. Together Alpha and the UWGT facilitator agreed that strategic planning would best encapsulate several of these areas of development. The UWGT facilitator recommended a consultant from the CBCI technical assistance team for this work. After interviewing the consultant, Alpha agreed she was the right person for the job. One of the reasons for the match, beyond her skills as a consultant, was that given the racial demographics of the community and previous challenges with bringing in outside expertise, the executive director and the UWGT staff believed it was important to have a strong, skilled woman of color leading a process that would involve doing needs assessments of the community.

Challenges arose just a few weeks following the match. Alpha's executive director called the UWGT staff person in confidence to indicate that a key board member, who had tacitly agreed to the decision to undertake strategic planning, was actually opposed to it and was even making attempts to undermine it. Given that Alpha was in the midst of a challenging partnership to deliver more services to newcomers in the area, the board member thought strategic planning was too theoretical and that the real area of work should be operations. The UWGT facilitator led a problem-solving meeting with the consulting team and Alpha's executive director. The group agreed on a new approach, drawing on the strengths of the group. The approach consisted of three new tactics: 1) the strategic planning consultant would take a step back from the actual process and play more of a coaching role with the board member individually, focusing on what the group felt were the board member's concerns and areas of resistance; 2) the UWGT facilitator would provide training in board governance, focusing on board and staff roles and responsibilities; and 3) a third member of the technical assistance team would focus on the service-delivery partnership and begin to develop some protocols and templates for partnership planning.

A few weeks following this intervention, the strategic planning consultant called the UWGT staff person to report that she and the board member had agreed to a special session for the board on the planning process. The consultant said that the board member was comfortable with the plan for a forty-five minute session. This session would involve checking in about any concerns on what's happening, how people are feeling, what are some of the issues people are grappling with, and what might challenge the implementation of the strategic plan.

Following this team-based intervention and rearrangement of the capacity building plan, the process proceeded successfully to the conclusion of the strategic planning. In an evaluation interview, another board member summed up what he learned: "Strategic planning used to be something I saw as 'we have to do it.' My attitude was we just have to 'chunk down and do it.' But when we started the process, some people had very different perspectives on what Alpha was and what we should be doing. It took lots of discussion to refine these different points of view. All of these things we want to do are important, but it is more important to focus on our strengths—*to be strategic*. The needs are so great we can't be everything to everybody."

Description of the practice

The practice we employed was *high engagement, team-based consulting* with a team leader based at United Way. This practice had three key characteristics: 1) cultural competence, 2) adaptive capacity, and 3) helpful oversight by a funder with a capacity building mandate.

First, each member of the consulting team was specifically recruited for his or her cross-cultural competence, cross-functional capabilities, and his or her common belief in the intrinsic right of communities to self-determination. This value is best exemplified in the words of a newcomer leader, "Empower people to take charge of solutions for themselves." This piloted practice of emphasizing cultural competence rather than cultural specificity (matching a consultant based on skills and ethno-racial background) was borne out in the preliminary evaluation of the CBCI project, which indicated that in the opinion of participants, a general competence and openness to cultural diversity is more important than culturally specific knowledge of particular populations.

Second, a majority of the team members, including the UWGT staff person, had experience working in social service organizations. This meant that while each team member had certain areas of specialization such as strategic planning or financial management, each also had generalist capabilities. They also understood the reality of the organizations that serve diverse, high-need populations; such organizations are small, underfunded, and lack infrastructure. The combination of experience and generalist skills translated into consultants with high degrees of adaptive capacity. Rather than functioning as narrow technical assistance experts, these individuals had varied skill sets and varied approaches to technical assistance delivery; they could respond as the occasion demanded. They could be coaches, mediators, facilitators, and problem solvers.

Finally, the team was facilitated by a UWGT staff person functionally separate from UWGT's funding process. This individual had problem-solving skills, was capable of augmenting the technical assistance skills of the consulting team, and had a good network of resources, tools, and connections. In a large part, this network of resources, tools and connections came about because, as a staff person in a funding institution doing capacity building work, she had a number of advantages: a broad overview of capacity issues facing the sector, including the need for unique approaches to capacity building for organizations serving immigrants and refugees; access to a wide pool of technical assistance consultants from which to select the most skilled individuals; and the power of working in a widely known and respected funding institution. She was able, as evidenced in other aspects of the project, to call someone and get something done when challenges arose or there were positive connections to be made. Perhaps most importantly, the staff person had supported a number of capacity development initiatives at Alpha over several years, was trusted by Alpha's executive director and senior staff, and was familiar to its board.

The practice of high engagement, team-based consulting grew out of observations of the challenging nature of the environment in which organizations serving newcomer communities exist—environmental challenges that other organizations may face, but hardly to the same degree. Challenges specific to organizations serving newcomer populations include: new populations requiring services and support can emerge rapidly due to changing international conditions; organizations serving newcomers exist in a climate of little to no funding for organizational infrastructure, unless the population is a long-established one; and a general lack of understanding on behalf of many mainstream institutions of the cultural differences among diverse populations, resulting in a "one size fits all" approach to capacity building.

Analysis

The following factors helped make this practice effective with the CBCI program:

- *Use consulting teams rather than individual consultants.* A team-based approach allows for the variety of skills, methods, and approaches required by smaller organizations, which lack strong systems to bolster themselves against environmental fluctuations.

- *Recruit consultants who know the territory.* Use consultants who have experience working with immigrant- and refugee-serving nonprofits or who are immigrant or refugee leaders themselves. Nothing takes the place of being able to relate to the client because you yourself have walked in their shoes.

- *Use a diverse, culturally competent consulting team, prioritizing cultural competency over cultural specificity.* Such an approach ensures that skills and experience are the first priority in assigning consultants while at the same time recognizes that being able to work across racial differences is a key component of the multiracial nature of our urban context.

- *Cultivate funders' ability to engage in, or support, capacity building as part of their mandate to grantees.* This allows the community to take advantage of funders' capabilities as networkers, connectors, and resources.

Case Study Summary

As capacity building practitioners, we thought that sharing examples of our own work would be the most valuable thing we could offer to our colleagues. These case studies represent a snapshot of the complex and evolving practices that have proven effective in our work with immigrant- and refugee-led organizations. They are good evidence of the great variety of capacity building approaches at work, but they also illustrate some very common themes: cultural competence, trust, asset-based capacity building, participatory practices, and the need to be highly flexible are among those. We hope that these cases will help others as they engage with immigrant- and refugee-led organizations.

CHAPTER THREE

LESSONS LEARNED

There are important lessons in the Nexus Project for everyone concerned with immigrant- and refugee-led organizations, including funders, IRLO leaders, and all manner of capacity builders.

Here we describe three broad lessons with implications for all of those groups. Following that, we list the implications for each group. Finally, we note some lessons about peer learning for capacity builders, drawn from our own experience in the Nexus Project.

1. **Effective capacity building takes time, which requires resources.**
   No one can do good capacity building work without adequate time. This is true for nonprofit organizations as well as for capacity builders. It is particularly true in capacity building with IRLOs, which demands time for quality relationship building, for complex dynamics and changing circumstances, and for leadership development. Lack of time and resources is a serious barrier for IRLOs, which are often small, under-resourced, and embedded in communities with limited access to resources.

2. **More immigrant and refugee capacity builders are needed.**
   We know that cultural identity and cultural "fluency" are important in capacity building; that experience with immigrant and refugee organizations helps; and that culture, language, and power differences can be barriers to capacity building. Supporting and developing more capacity builders from immigrant and refugee backgrounds will strengthen IRLOs as well as capacity building organizations. It will also increase the access of IRLOs and immigrant and refugee communities to resources and power.

3. **Capacity builders need continuous learning and development.**
   To be most effective, capacity builders working with IRLOs have to be engaged in continuous learning about themselves, their practice, and about the contexts of the organizations they serve. Capacity builders need time and opportunities for reflection, sharing, and peer learning within and across organizations.

LESSONS LEARNED

1. Effective capacity building takes time, which requires resources.

2. More immigrant and refugee capacity builders are needed.

3. Capacity builders need continuous learning and development.

Implications for the funding community:

- Fund it! Support IRLO capacity building with the funding it needs.
- Fund capacity building over the long term.
- Ensure that IRLOs drive their capacity building work.
- Support the development of more capacity builders from immigrant and refugee communities.
- Encourage peer learning among both IRLOs and capacity builders.
- Support continuous learning and development among capacity builders.

Implications for IRLO leaders:

- Do it! Find the resources and support you need to build your organization's capacity.
- Work with capacity building practitioners who are right for you and your situation.
- Stay in control of the process.
- Learn from your peers and share your expertise with them.
- Encourage staff, board, and volunteers to develop their own skills as capacity builders.

Implications for capacity building providers:

- Allow enough time and ensure enough resources to do effective capacity building work with IRLOs.
- Make the right match of people, skills, and experience.
- Develop more immigrant and refugee practitioners.
- Budget adequate time and space for learning.

Lessons about peer learning for capacity builders:

- The process of peer learning and reflection is critical to our own development.
- Face-to-face meetings and relationship building are necessary components of peer learning.
- Participatory peer learning methods are most engaging and fruitful.
- Participatory design is important.
- Peer learning takes time!

Implications for the funding community

Effective IRLO capacity building increases the ability of both IRLOs and their communities to achieve their goals and shape their futures. Following are implications of our lessons for funders who want to support immigrants and refugees:

- *Fund it! Support IRLO capacity building with the funding it needs.* Both IRLOs and capacity builders need real resources if they are to do effective capacity building. IRLOs are already doing much more than they are funded to do. IRLOs need support for capacity building as well as operating support grants. Funding for capacity building must also account for the investment that capacity builders make in building relationships with IRLOs.

- *Fund capacity building over the long term.* IRLOs and capacity builders need multiple-year timeframes to build capacity effectively and sustainably. We need adequate time to engage people, to plan and implement change, and to learn from the process. Invest in holistic initiatives, rather than piecemeal efforts.

- *Ensure that IRLOs drive their capacity building work.* IRLOs need choices in capacity building methods and providers. They need control over their own objectives and information. Capacity building that doesn't respond to IRLO needs will not be nearly as effective as capacity building that is driven by IRLOs' goals and preferences.

- *Support the development of more capacity builders from immigrant and refugee communities.* Fund initiatives and internship programs aimed at developing trainers, facilitators, organizers, and consultants from immigrant and refugee communities. Utilize immigrant capacity building providers, or capacity building organizations that have immigrants and refugees on staff or in their networks.

- *Support continuous learning and development among capacity builders.* Capacity building practitioners also need resources to build their own capacity, through peer learning, training, and other development opportunities. Provide operating support grants to nonprofit capacity builders and fund initiatives that include professional development support for practitioners.

- *Encourage peer learning among both IRLOs and capacity builders.* Provide both groups with resources and opportunities to come together and learn from one another.

Implications for IRLO leaders

In our interviews, we heard from IRLO leaders encouraging other IRLO leaders to do capacity building, because of the difference it can make for their organizations and communities.

- *Do it! Find the resources and support you need to build your organization's capacity.* Effective capacity building can increase your ability to meet your mission and build your community's power.

- *Work with capacity building practitioners who are right for you and your situation.* This may or may not mean someone from your own cultural community. Find practitioners you can work well with and who can support you in achieving your objectives.

- *Stay in control of the process.* Claim your voice and power and don't be afraid to make changes if things aren't going well. Capacity building should meet *your* needs and build on *your* assets. At the same time, be open-minded and flexible about your plans as new information emerges.

- *Learn from your peers and share your expertise with them.* Immigrant and refugee leaders can build the capacity of IRLOs and other organizations by sharing experience, coaching and training others, and working together toward shared goals.

- *Encourage staff, board, and volunteers to develop their own skills as capacity builders.* Identify leaders who may have the right kind of skills, experience, and passion to get started as a trainer, facilitator, technical assistance provider, or consultant. Connect them with opportunities to gain training and experience either internally or externally.

Implications for capacity building providers

In addition to the many practitioner implications noted in Chapter 2, capacity building providers—management support organizations, facilitators, technical assistance providers, consultants, and others—should keep the following in mind:

- *Allow enough time and ensure enough resources to do effective capacity building work with IRLOs.* Take this into account in planning, budgeting, and in business models. Many organizations doing significant work with IRLOs fund at least some of their work with IRLOs through something other than consulting fees.

- *Make the right match of people, skills, and experience.* Organizations or networks that can access a diverse pool of practitioners, including immigrants and refugees, are more likely to be able to make those matches.

- *Develop more immigrant and refugee practitioners.* This means increasing the number of immigrants and refugees in consulting pools and employing them in management support organizations. It also means targeting immigrants and refugees for training opportunities, partnering with them, mentoring them, and promoting them.

- *Budget adequate time and space for learning.* Invest in continuous learning and development in order to do the best work. This includes personal and professional reflection, learning about immigrant organizations and communities, and developing relevant technical skills and knowledge. Share what you learn with networks of colleagues both inside and across organizations. Find opportunities to reflect together with IRLO leaders.

Lessons about Peer Learning for Capacity Builders

In our own peer learning journey as capacity builders, we also learned some more specific lessons about this approach to learning and development.

- *The process of peer learning and reflection is critical to our own development.* We all have busy lives and multiple professional responsibilities; it is difficult to carve out time for individual and collective reflection, and to learn from one another. But when we do, we recognize how valuable it can be for us and for our practice.

- *Face-to-face meetings and relationship building are necessary components of peer learning.* We need time together to learn about each other and the work that each of us does. (In the Nexus Project, we found that we needed to understand our commonalities to fully engage as peers.) Only after building relationships and a base of shared understanding can we fully benefit from less intensive peer learning activities such as conference calls and email exchanges.

- *Participatory peer learning methods are most engaging and fruitful.* One of the best things we did in the Nexus Project was our initial sharing of the stories that later became the case studies above. Open and inclusive facilitation of peer learning is also important.

- *Participatory design is important.* Capacity builders know the importance of process design and are skilled at it. Designing our own learning experience is the best way to make sure we get the most out of it.

- *Peer learning takes time!* We did not have enough time together, especially face to face, to do all we set out to do.

Continuing the Journey

The lessons above present major challenges to all of us who care about IRLOs and immigrant communities. We must rise to the challenge: find the resources, bring more immigrants and refugees into the capacity building field, and make room for practitioner reflection and development. We need:

- *More providers* from immigrant and refugee communities, with broad and deep skills. This will require substantial investments in training and development.

- *More outreach* to other grantmakers and capacity builders to educate them on the needs of IRLOs and their communities.

- *More intensive, structured peer learning* to connect those doing capacity building in local areas, who are often working in isolation from peers across the country.

- *More research and inquiry* into capacity building approaches that are either universal or appropriate in specific IRLO settings.

There are other questions we as capacity builders still need to wrestle with. For example, what do organizational lifecycle or development stages mean for grassroots organizations? How can IRLOs best shape their organizational structure to serve their interests? When or where does a consultancy model fit for IRLOs? Can capacity building with IRLOs be done effectively by an individual provider?

We suggested some ideas about cultural competence for capacity builders in this report. We are aware that this is an ongoing conversation among capacity builders, one in which we will continue to participate. We also want to participate with others in elaborating what it means for us as capacity builders to act as allies to IRLOs.

Finally, at the end of the Nexus Project, we began to ask each other how we can best share what we learned with our colleagues, beginning within our own organizations. We still need to share and implement effective practices for peer learning among capacity builders.

The context for IRLOs in North America will continue to evolve. Changing government policies and shifting political winds will affect the resources available to each IRLO, as well as relationships among immigrant and refugee communities and the larger community. We remain committed to doing the most effective work we can to support IRLOs in achieving their goals and building their communities. Though the Nexus Project has ended, it was only one leg of our shared journey. We look forward to continuing along the way with you.

APPENDICES

APPENDIX 1

FACTORS IN SUCCESSFUL CAPACITY BUILDING WITH IMMIGRANT- AND REFUGEE-LED ORGANIZATIONS (IRLOS)

What follows is a summary of three stages of research done as part of the Nexus Project: a preliminary literature review and two sets of interviews with capacity builders and immigrant- and refugee-led organizations (IRLOs). This research was conducted by Wilder Research Center in 2004–2005.

An initial literature review by Wilder Research focused broadly on capacity building with immigrant- and refugee-led organizations. Next, Fieldstone Alliance gathered qualitative information about capacity building efforts by conducting telephone interviews with Nexus capacity builders and the IRLOs they had worked with. In a second set of interviews, Wilder Research gathered qualitative information from the Nexus partners (or a capacity building consultant they provided) and a second set of IRLOs with whom those partners had worked on a capacity building project. This time, the capacity builders completed a self-administered survey, and the IRLOs completed interviews by telephone. The types of capacity building covered in both sets of interviews primarily concerned basic nonprofit management and board responsibilities, furthering constituency leadership development, and implementation of particular organizational processes.

The immigrant- and refugee-led organizations interviewed for this study find their capacity building project experiences worth the time and energy they invested. Most say their organizations have grown in important ways as a result of the capacity building activities, well beyond even the stated objectives of the projects. These benefits include increased confidence in their own capabilities and perspectives, increased recognition by their communities, and increased comfort with asserting their own viewpoints and needs when working with consultants and mainstream institutions.

The factors described below are divided into two major categories: those derived from the literature on capacity building with IRLOs, and those derived from the interviews with IRLOs.

Success Factors Described in the Literature

In general: Effective capacity building in IRLOs requires sufficient assistance over a period of years and funding to support the entire period of capacity building as well as follow-up support. Peer learning and hands-on training approaches work best.

For IRLOs: Stable leadership and operations, along with the time, energy, and commitment to engage in the process, are important success factors for capacity building. Preliminary assessment of an IRLO's strengths and weaknesses is highly recommended.

For capacity builders: To work effectively with IRLOs, providers must have not only organizational expertise but also the ability to create an affirming, culturally sensitive, responsive, and productive relationship with the IRLO. This relationship should be based on the capacity builder's experience with, knowledge of, and sensitivity to the IRLO and its community's culture, norms, experiences, and challenges. Effective capacity builders also understand that within immigrant and refugee communities, learning activities may be viewed by the IRLO as a valuable form of community (not just organizational) capacity building, which can further social equity for the community as a whole.

Success Factors Derived from Interviews Conducted for this Study

Factors related to the quality of the IRLO/capacity builder relationship

While capacity builders often attribute their success to specific expertise and activities, IRLOs more often attribute success to the capacity builder's deep commitment to their organization and community and to the quality of the relationship created by the capacity builder, making it possible for the IRLO to fully accept and use the assistance being offered. Effective capacity builders think and act as allies to the IRLOs, developing a relationship that is much more personal and engaged than the traditional "consultant" model.

Capacity builders who are perceived as "allies" incorporate these approaches to the work:

- Putting significant effort into learning about the history, culture, issues, experiences, and challenges of this particular IRLO and its community (a step beyond what is often considered basic "cultural competence") prior to beginning any work—demonstrating an ongoing "fierce commitment to learning."

- Being flexible—willing to play multiple overlapping roles and adapting activities to the IRLO's specific needs and/or limitations.

- Using words and actions that show a commitment to partnering rather than "teaching." In other words, acting in ways that show the IRLO that they and their perspectives are of value and thinking and speaking in terms of "we" rather than "I" and "you."

- Advocating for the IRLO and directly linking them to resources, such as setting up meetings with mainstream funders and institutions, accompanying the IRLO to the meetings, and following up with the resource contact to ensure a positive outcome.

- Interacting with the IRLO in ways that are inclusive of, open to, and respectful of all perspectives and decision-making processes, balanced with providing the IRLO with a neutral and objective "outsider" point of view.

- Being "fluent about power" in relationships involving organizations, communities, and institutions; putting it "on the table" as an issue for open discussion, and ensuring that people with limited English fluency are able to fully engage in all discussions and decision-making.

Factors related to activities

- Effective capacity building has specific and explicit objectives, which may require the capacity builder to spend a great deal of time coaching and supporting the IRLO as it articulates its goals and how those goals might be met.

- Successful capacity building also requires revisiting the original objectives and related activities repeatedly throughout the course of the project, with all those involved, to make sure they all are still in agreement and that expectations are being met.

- Effective training with IRLOs combines learning with immediate and repeated hands-on use of the new skills, processes, and tools.

"…By working with this project, the confidence of who we are and what we are about has increased dramatically. We were fearful of where we didn't have expertise. This project showed where we had expertise and how this was transferable."

"If you have the opportunity to do capacity building, seize it. It is great work that never gets done because of a lack of capacity, which can make a vicious circle— you don't grow because you don't have a plan."

— from IRLO interviews

Factors related to the capacity and resources of the capacity builder

- IRLOs value skilled and knowledgeable capacity builders who have experience with similar organizations and who also have connections to resources.

- Effective capacity building in IRLOs requires providing the financial resources necessary to free key actors to participate in the capacity building activities. This "buying time" is especially important in IRLOs that represent newcomer communities and small IRLOs that might have little or no paid staff and a volunteer board (most of whom have full-time jobs of their own) doing the essential work of the IRLO.

Factors that Hamper Success

During interviews conducted for this study, IRLOs described three main factors that can impede successful capacity building:

- Lack of flexibility in structured programs or initiatives for capacity building—required designs or templates with restricted timelines and/or choice in capacity building consultants.

- Disruptions or constraints in funding—late funding, the unexpected end of funding prior to the end of the project, changes in rules about who receives funding and how, and inflexible rules about how funding can be spent.

- An IRLO's perception that the capacity builder is biased or has deliberately excluded some stakeholder(s) by using complex professional language and jargon; by providing translation assistance in multi-ethnic IRLOs to some groups but not others; or by favoring or leaving out some stakeholders when soliciting input during an assessment.

APPENDIX 2

ANNOTATED BIBLIOGRAPHY

Alliance for Nonprofit Management. *2002 Regional Meetings Chicago and West Palm Beach: Funding and Capacity Building in Difficult Times and Focus on Rural, Under-Served, and Minority-Led Nonprofits.* Summary report of two meetings, Alliance for Nonprofit Management, 2002. http://www.allianceonline.org/events_and_announcements. ipage/alliance_regional_meetings.page/2002_regional_meetings.file

Suggestions about how to develop the quality relationship that is essential for good capacity building within four dimensions: assessment, technical assistance and consultation, skills transfer and development, and coaching and peer-to-peer learning.

Asian Pacific American Legal Center. *Crossing Boundaries: An Exploration of Effective Leadership Development in Communities.* Los Angeles: Asian Pacific American Legal Center, 2003. http://www.apalc.org/crossing_boundaries.pdf

The report highlights training programs for leaders to teach them to skillfully cross boundaries in a variety of ways.

Backer, Tom, Jane Ellen Bleeg, and Kathryn Groves. *The Expanding Universe: New Directions in Nonprofit Capacity Building.* Washington, DC: Alliance for Nonprofit Management, 2004. http://www.allianceonline.org/publications/expanding_universe.page

This research study reveals leading edge capacity building work, highlighting innovative strategies in strengthening nonprofit organizations via intermediaries, grantmakers, community based nonprofits, and individual philanthropists. This research, done by Human Interaction Research Institute, considerably expands our understanding of the broad array of actors and the strategies they use to build capacity with nonprofits.

Brooks Masters, Suzette, and Ted Permutter. *Networking the Networks: Improving Information Flows in the Immigration Field.* New York: The International Center for Migration, Ethnicity and Citizenship at New School University, 2001. http://www.gcir.org/resources/bibliography/NetworkingTheNetworks.pdf

This sixty-page report analyzes the immigration-related information resource needs of over 120 immigrant advocacy and service organizations around the country. It also analyzes the methods used by these groups to obtain and impart information.

Center for Nonprofit Management in Southern California. *Building the Capacity of Community Organizations in Los Angeles County.* Los Angeles: Center for Nonprofit Management in Southern California, 1998. http://www.cnmsocal.org/AboutNonprofits/capacitybuilding.html

An assessment of the management development needs of nonprofits with moderate and small budgets.

Cohen, Eric, Juliette Steadman, and Rufus Whitley. *Immigrant Leadership Training Curriculum, 2000 edition.* San Francisco: Immigrant Legal Resource Center, 2000. http://www.ilrc.org/onlineresource.php

This handbook chronicles the leadership development model explored in a joint initiative of Lutheran Immigration and Refugee Service and the Immigrant Legal Resource Center. The curriculum employs interactive teaching techniques with the goal of helping dedicated community leaders develop and refine their leadership and advocacy skills, use such skills in their communities to work on civic issues, and build alliances with community-based organizations.

The Colorado Trust. *Helping Immigrants and Refugees in Colorado: Programs Funded by The Colorado Trust's Supporting Immigrants and Refugee Families Initiative.* Denver, CO: The Colorado Trust, 2002. http://www.coloradotrust.org/repository/publications/pdfs/SIRFIgranteesbrochure.pdf

The Trust's Supporting Immigrant and Refugee Families Initiative and programs of twenty-three initiative grantees are listed and described in this publication. Contact information for the grantee organizations is also included.

Connolly, Paul, and Carol Lukas. *Strengthening Nonprofit Performance: A Funder's Guide to Capacity Building.* St. Paul, MN: Fieldstone Alliance, Inc., 2002.

This book synthesizes the most recent capacity building practice and research into a collection of strategies, steps, and examples funders can use to strengthen nonprofits. This book can be purchased at http://www.FieldstoneAlliance.org

Connolly, Paul, and Peter York. *Building the Capacity of Capacity Builders: A Study of Management Support and Field-Building Organizations in the Nonprofit Sector.* With the assistance of Sally Munemitsu, Catalina Ruiz-Healy, Anne Sherman and Cindy Trebb. New York: TCC Group, 2003. http://www.tccgrp.com/pdfs/buildingthecapacityofcapacitybuilders.pdf

This report is based on a study of capacity builders (primarily management support organizations). The report looks at capacity building needs within management support organizations and other intermediaries in the nonprofit sector. It also discusses effective capacity building methods for both intermediaries and nonprofit organizations.

De Lucca, Alison. *Rising with the Tide: Capacity Building Strategies for Small, Emerging Immigrant Organizations*. Los Angeles: Los Angeles Immigrant Funders' Collaborative, 2002.

This report explores how to increase the effectiveness of small, emerging immigrant groups and assists the Los Angeles Immigrant Funders' Collaborative in deciding how to strategically invest in building the capacity of these small groups in Los Angeles County. This report is available by e-mailing Grantmakers Concerned with Immigrant and Refugees.

De Vita, Carol J., and Cory Fleming, eds. *Building Capacity in Nonprofit Organizations*. Washington, DC: The Urban Institute, 2001. http://www.urban.org/pdfs/building_capacity.pdf

A report on capacity building framework and strategies for organizations and foundation initiatives.

Doherty, Susan, and Steven E. Mayer, Ph.D. *Results of an Inquiry into Capacity Building Programs for Nonprofit Programs*. Minneapolis: Effective Communities Project, 2003. http://www.effectivecommunities.com/ECP_CapacityBuildingInquiry.pdf

This report discusses capacity building at the nonprofit organization level. It describes different aspects and elements for effective capacity building work.

DuPraw, Marcelle E., and Marya Axner. Working on Common Cross-cultural Communication Challenges. The AMPU web site, Produced by Arcadia Pictures in association with PBS Onlines, 1997. http://www.pbs.org/ampu/crosscult.html

This web site is an online guide for improving communication with a multicultural lens. It provides a practical framework for understanding and respecting cultural differences.

Dyer-Ives Foundation. *New Neighbors, New Opportunities: Immigrants and Refugees in Grand Rapids*. Grand Rapids, MI: Dyer-Ives Foundation, 2003. http://www.dyer-ives.org/newneighbors/

This short publication addresses the importance of strengthening immigrant and refugee communities' systems of support: organizations and programs, leadership development, and capacity development.

Festen, Marcia, and Marianne Philbin. *How Effective Nonprofits Work: A Guide for Donors, Board Members and Foundation Officers*. Chicago: Giving Greater Chicago, 2002.

This practical guide is designed to help donors, board members, and foundation officers quickly familiarize themselves with the strategies, structures, tactics, and best practices that contribute to the development of healthy nonprofit organizations. This guide can be purchased at http://www.givingforum.org/resources/publications_effective_cover.html

Gantz McKay, Emily, and Kristin Scotchmer, Mary Ellen Ros, and Myriam Figueroa. *Immigrant and Refugee-Led Organizations and their Technical Assistance Needs*. Report prepared for the Ford Foundation, Mosaica, 2001. http://mosaica.coure-tech.com/resources/ford.pdf

This report summarizes the work and results of the Immigrant and Refugee-Led Organizations Project, analyzing the technical assistance needs and experiences of immigrant- and refugee-led organizations. It also recommends guiding principles, models, and processes for providing technical assistance to such entities.

Gantz McKay, Emily, Kristin Scotchmer, Myriam Figueroa-Melendez, and Saima Huq. *Research on Barriers and Opportunities for Increasing Leadership in Immigrant and Refugee Communities*. Report prepared for the Hyams Foundation, Mosaica, 2000. http://mosaica.coure-tech.com/resources/Full%20Hyams%20report.pdf

This study, carried out by Mosaica: The Center for Nonprofit Development and Pluralism, was undertaken in 1999 to assist the Hyams Foundation in deciding how its grantmaking in civic participation might best be used to increase the exercise and development of leadership in immigrants and refugees. The study identifies barriers, opportunities, and best practices. It found that effective leadership programs typically have a strong community base and are designed to reflect the needs of the specific communities. It also identifies numerous factors that contribute to effective grantmaking in this field. To obtain a hard copy of the report, contact the Hyams Foundation at 617-426-5600.

Guerra, Luz. *Technical Assistance and Progressive Organizations for Social Change in Communities of Color: A Report to the Saguarao Grantmaking Board of the Funding Exchange*. New York: Funding Exchange, 1999.

This document is part of the Working Papers series for COMM_ORG: The Online Conference on Community Organizing and Development at http://comm-org.wisc.edu/papers.htm

Ho, Mimi, et al. *Mapping the Immigrant Infrastructure*. Executive summary prepared for the Annie E. Casey Foundation, Applied Research Center, 2002. http://www.arc.org/content/view/243/48/

This report includes an examination of models of immigrant and refugee organizations, a compilation of data from interviews with over 120 key leaders, case studies of 6 local organizations, and an assessment of the effect of the post-September 11 political environment on immigrant and refugee communities.

Holley, Lynn Carol. "Ethnic Agencies in Communities of Color: A Study of Missions, Services, Structures, and Capacity Building Needs." Dissertation, University of Washington, 1998.

This paper includes summaries from immigrant and refugee leaders who listed their priority areas for training, types of training, desired trainer characteristics, and ideas of successful strategies. It also recommends skill-building areas for consultants and useful strategies for increasing the effectiveness of mainstream agencies in meeting the technical assistance needs of communities of color.

Hyunhye Cho, Eunice, Francisco Arguelles Paz y Puente, Miriam Ching Yoon Louie, and Sasha Khokha. *Bridge: Building a Race and Immigration Dialogue in the Global Economy.* Oakland, CA: National Network for Immigrant and Refugee Rights, 2004.

This is a practical, popular education resource for immigrant and refugee community organizers around the topic of immigration. Related handouts and worksheets available in Spanish and Korean. This book can be purchased at http://www.nnirr.org/projects/projects_bridge.html

Jacobs, Bruce. *Echoes from the Field: Proven Capacity-Building Principles for Nonprofits.* Washington, DC: Environmental Support Center and Innovation Network, Inc, 2002. http://www.envsc.org/bestpractices.pdf

This research report highlights a set of core criteria for effectiveness and excellence that enable providers to strengthen nonprofits.

Lodwick, Dora. *Supporting Immigrant and Refugee Families Initiative Outcome Evaluation Feasibility Study.* Executive Summary, The Colorado Trust, 2002. http://www.coloradotrust.org/repository/publications/pdfs/SIRFIevalfeasibilityrpt04.pdf

This report shows the feasibility of gathering outcome data at the client level of the Trust's Supporting Immigrant and Refugee Families Initiative and what the requirements and strategies of such an evaluation might be. The publication details the findings and recommendations of the feasibility study. Call 303-837-1200 to request a printed copy.

McGarvey, Craig. *Pursuing Democracy's Promise: Newcomer Civic Participation in America.* Sebastopol, CA: Grantmakers Concerned with Immigrants and Refugees in collaboration with the Funders' Committee on Civic Participation, 2004. http://www.discountfoundation.org/pdf/pursuing_democracys_promise.pdf

This report highlights the refugees' and immigrants' stories of engagement and participation in public affairs. There are several examples of immigrant and refugee integration with and contributions to their local communities through their civic participation process. The report gives context for immigrant and refugee movements and the relationship with nonprofits and philanthropy.

National Network for Immigrant and Refugee Rights. *Uprooted: Refugees of the Global Economy*, Video. With Sasha Khokha, Ulla Nilsen, Jon Fromer, and Francisco Herrera. Oakland, CA: National Network for Immigrant and Refugee Rights, 2001.

This 28-minute video documentary weaves together the stories of three immigrants into a compelling tale of how the global economy (including U.S. corporations and the International Monetary Fund) has forced immigrants to leave their home countries. The video can be purchased at http://www.nnirr.org/get/get_video.html

Newman, Audrey. *Built to Change: Catalytic Capacity-Building in Nonprofit Organization*. A sabbatical report submitted to The David and Lucile Packard Foundation and The Nature Conservancy, 2001. http://conserveonline.org/workspaces/apcpal/tools/Audrey%20Newman%20Sabbatical%20Report.doc

The author offers a framework for understanding capacity building efforts beyond traditional venues of assessments, workshops, training manuals. Her studies are focused on small organizations creating an environment of life long learning and change.

Nonprofit Assistance Center. *Refugee and Immigrant Collaborations: Best Practices Research Summary*. Seattle, WA: Nonprofit Assistance Center and the Northwest Area Foundation, 2003.

Summary of qualities and factors for successful collaboration that is grounded in community knowledge, including cultural values and behaviors. Available online to Alliance for Nonprofit Management members or contact NAC at 206-324-5850 or http://www.NACSeattle.org

Pendleton, Gail. *Building the Rhythm of Change: Developing Leadership and Improving Services within the Battered Rural Immigrant Women's Community*. San Francisco, CA: The Family Violence Prevention Fund. http://www.endabuse.org/programs/immigrant/files/Rhythm.pdf

Geared primarily for domestic violence service providers focusing on advancing the rights of battered immigrant women and improving their access to services, the manual may also be useful for other organizations or individuals advocating for immigrants' legal rights.

Pittz, Will, and Rinku Sen. *Short Changed: Foundation Giving and Communities of Color*. Oakland, CA: Applied Research Center, 2004. http://www.arc.org/content/view/271/48/

This research report, by Applied Research Center, describes funding trends and how they impact communities of color, immigrants, and refugees.

REFT Institute, Inc. *Keys to Cultural Competency: A Literature Review for Evaluators of Recent Immigrant and Refugee Service Programs in Colorado*. Denver, CO: The Colorado Trust, 2002. http://www.colorado-trust.org/repository/publications/pdfs/KeystoCulturalCompetency04.pdf

This publication details unique characteristics of nine separate cultures (including people from Bosnia-Herzegovina, Kurdistan, the former Soviet Union, Central America, Mexico, Laos, Vietnam, Somalia, and Sudan), and related implications for conducting research and evaluation within these cultures. Call 303-837-1200 to request a printed copy of the report.

Sayre, Kiki. *Guidelines and Best Practices for Culturally Competent Evaluations*. Denver, CO: The Colorado Trust, 2002. http://coloradotrust.org/repository/publications/pdfs/GuidelinesBestPracticesCulturally04.pdf

As Colorado's population continues to become more ethnically diverse, The Trust believes that evaluators need additional tools so that they can employ appropriate strategies, gather valid data across diverse groups of people, and show sensitivity to the diverse populations being served. This report is a summary of two workshops that focused on providing evaluators with these tools. Call 303-837-1200 to request a printed copy.

United Nations High Commissioner for Refugees. *The State of the World's Refugees 2000*. Cambridge, MA: Oxford University Press, 2001. http://www.unhcr.org/pubs/sowr2000/prelims.pdf

Subtitled Fifty Years of Humanitarian Action, this report provides a historical overview and critical analysis of the first fifty years of the work of the United Nations High Commission for Refugees. The final chapter describes the global situation and changing dynamics for refugees at the beginning of the 21st century.

Wildau, Rich, and Gurudev Khalsa. *Providing Technical Assistance to Build Organizational Capacity*. Denver, CO: The Colorado Trust, 2002. http://www.coloradotrust.org/repository/publications/pdfs/TAforSIRFI.pdf

This publication provides an overview of the technical assistance offered to grantees under The Colorado Trust's Supporting Immigrant and Refugee Families Initiative (SIRFI). Lessons learned and recommendations for other organizations offering technical assistance also are detailed within this report. The Organizational Assessment Process—a tool developed to help identify, design and deliver the appropriate technical assistance to SIRFI grantees—is included in the report. Call 303-837-1200 to request a printed copy.

Wilder Research Center. *Speaking for Themselves: A Survey of Hispanic, Hmong, Russian, and Somali Immigrants in Minneapolis-St. Paul.* St. Paul, MN: Amherst H. Wilder Foundation, 2000. http://www.nfg.org/otherpubs/SpeakingForThemselves.pdf

This survey illuminates some common themes in the immigrant story, highlighting important nuances for the wave of immigration to the Twin Cities area.

Organizational Resources

Alliance for Nonprofit Management

This organization maintains a reservoir of resources about cultural competency in nonprofit work. These resources are relevant to nonprofit leadership and management, capacity building for nonprofit effectiveness, and the work of transforming the sector to generate large-scale change. http://www.allianceonline.org/about/cc_resources.page

Center for Immigration Studies

The Center for Immigration Studies is an independent, non-partisan nonprofit research organization founded in 1985. It is the nation's only think tank devoted exclusively to research and policy analysis of the economic, social, demographic, fiscal, and other impacts of immigration on the United States. http://www.cis.org

Grantmakers Concerned with Immigrants and Refugees (GCIR)

GCIR's annotated, online bibliography includes more than 300 publications relating to immigrants and refugees from 2001 to the present. Pre-2001 publications may be found in the archive section under each category. The bibliography is organized according into several categories. http://www.gcir.org/resources/bibliography/leadership_and_capacity.htm

The Migration Policy Institute

The Migration Policy Institute (MPI) is an independent, nonpartisan nonprofit think tank in Washington, DC, dedicated to the study of the movement of people worldwide. MPI provides analysis, development, and evaluation of migration and refugee policies at the local, national, and international levels. http://www.migrationinformation.org

Nexus Partner Organizations

The Center to Support Immigrant Organizing (CSIO)

Lincoln Plaza
89 South Street, 7th Floor
Boston, MA 02111

Phone: 617-742-5165
Fax: 617-227-5270

The mission of the Center to Support Immigrant Organizing (CSIO) is to strengthen the work of individuals, groups, organizations, and communities dedicated to organizing immigrants around the issues that affect their lives. CSIO's work is focused in the greater Boston area, southeastern Massachusetts, and Rhode Island. Since June 2000, CSIO has worked with a network of approximately seventy-five immigrant activists, leaders, organizers, and directors to develop programs that help overcome barriers to organizing in immigrant communities. The work of CSIO is grounded in participatory process, peer learning, and leadership development as the core engines of individual, organizational, and community transformation. CSIO has worked in the Asian, Latino, African, Brazilian, Irish, Cape Verdean, Haitian, and other communities to support immigrant organizers, immigrant organizations, and community/labor collaborations that promote immigrant rights. CSIO activities include convening and coordinating cross-community collaborations, facilitating peer learning groups, training, technical assistance, and organizational development.

Community Consulting Group, LLC

5008 Morgan Avenue South
Minneapolis, MN 55419

Phone: 612-926-0122
www.ccgpartnership.com

Community Consulting Group, LLC works with leaders in the nonprofit and government sectors to create and sustain positive change in our communities through

- *Planning and assessment. We design and facilitate planning processes that respect the organization's history, assess current realities, and foster creativity and insight for planning the future, resulting in constructive, cohesive plans.*

- *Board governance. We invigorate an organization's leaders and build a dynamic governing board that effectively moves the organization into the future*

- *Alliances. We assist organizations in forming alliances that make a difference, creating mutually beneficial relationships that strengthen all partners, accomplishing greater results than one organization or group could achieve alone.*

- *Community engagement. We develop processes that fit the unique needs of organizations and communities, and we inform and engage people in opportunities to design and act on joint projects for community improvement.*

CompassPoint Nonprofit Services

731 Market Street, Suite 200
San Francisco, CA 94103

Phone: 415-541-9000
Fax: 415-541-7708
www.CompassPoint.org

Founded in 1975, CompassPoint Nonprofit Services is the nation's premier consulting, training, and research firm focused exclusively on the nonprofit sector. With offices in San Francisco and the Silicon Valley, CompassPoint strives to increase nonprofits' effectiveness by providing the management tools and concepts vital to solving pressing social problems and affecting critical social change.

A nonprofit ourselves, we work with organizations in areas including nonprofit board development, fundraising, technology, strategic planning, finance, organizational change, and executive leadership. Each year over 4,000 nonprofit staff and volunteers attend our workshops and conferences and nearly 300 nonprofits choose us as their consultants. We are a university for nonprofit staff, a quality consulting partner to the sector, a research institution and think tank, and a community organizer.

Fieldstone Alliance, Inc.

60 Plato Boulevard, Suite 150
St. Paul, MN 55107

Phone: 651-556-4500
Fax: 651-556-4517
www.FieldstoneAlliance.org

The mission of Fieldstone Alliance is to strengthen the performance of the nonprofit sector. Fieldstone Alliance has a twenty-four year history of providing consulting, training, research, publishing, and other capacity building services that strengthen leadership, enhance organizational performance, increase foundation effectiveness, and build the capacity of networks and intermediaries that support the nonprofit sector. Formerly a part of Wilder Center for Communities (of the Amherst H. Wilder Foundation), it began working

with mutual assistance associations serving Southeast Asian refugee communities in the 1980s. Using its ability to provide practical tools and resources and strategically link the resources of multiple partners and delivery systems, Fieldstone Alliance initiated the Nexus Project to enhance skills and increase information flow and sharing of practice within the nonprofit sector.

Local Initiatives Support Corporation, Twin Cities (LISC)

570 Asbury Street, Suite 207
St. Paul, MN 55104

Phone: 651-265-2293
Fax: 651-649-1112
www.LISCnet.org

Twin Cities LISC was established in 1988 and serves the Minneapolis-St. Paul metropolitan area. It is part of a national nonprofit whose mission is to help resident-led, community-based organizations transform distressed communities and neighborhoods into healthy places to live, do business, work, and raise families.

LISC's primary focus is to build the financial and technical capacity of community-based development corporations (CDCs) to sponsor housing, economic, and social development appropriate to their communities. Twin Cities LISC dedicates significant resources to support promising CDCs, believing that over time the right combination of funding, technical assistance, and training can substantially build the capacity of CDCs to achieve large-scale change in their neighborhoods. LISC also offers programs designed to test promising new strategies and meet emerging needs in the local community development field. Finally, LISC constantly seeks to impact public policy and create an environment that champions the efforts of local community development organizations.

Management Assistance Program for Nonprofits (MAP for Nonprofits)

2233 University Avenue, Suite 360
St. Paul, MN 55114

Phone: 651-632-7228
Fax: 651-647-1369
www.MAPfornonprofits.org

MAP for Nonprofits was organized in 1980, placing its first volunteer in January of that year. It was first a program of the local United Way and became a separate nonprofit organization in 1984. MAP's purpose is to build the capacity of nonprofit organizations to achieve mission-driven results.

Since 1980, MAP has provided quality, affordable management consulting and board recruitment services to thousands of nonprofit groups. Service areas include marketing and communications, business planning, strategic planning, legal, accounting and technology. MAP primarily works with nonprofit organizations in the Greater Twin Cities Metropolitan Area of Minneapolis and St. Paul, Minnesota, but has provided services for organizations in other areas of the U.S., including New York, Phoenix, Washington DC, and Atlanta.

Mosaica: The Center for Nonprofit Development and Pluralism

1522 K Street Northwest, Suite 1130
Washington, DC 20005

Phone: 202-887-0620
Fax: 202-887-0812
www.mosaica.org

Mosaica is a multicultural nonprofit that provides tools to other nonprofits to build just, inclusive, and thriving communities and societies. Its special commitment is to strengthen and support entities committed to serving and empowering those whose voices are least likely to be heard when public policies are adopted and resources allocated.

A national organization established in 1994 in the District of Columbia, Mosaica

- *Helps nonprofit organizations become stronger and more effective through training and facilitation, individual consultation, evaluation, and easy-to-use "how to" guides*

- *Links the nonprofit, public, and private sectors in ways that strengthen local communities and enrich American society*

- *Helps individuals and groups develop the skills to bridge racial, ethnic, and economic differences and work effectively in multicultural societies*

The Nonprofit Assistance Center (NAC)

1618 South Lane Street, Suite 201
Seattle, WA 98144

Phone: 206-324-5850
www.NACSeattle.org

The Nonprofit Assistance Center (NAC) is a social change organization that supports communities of color, low income, refugee, immigrant, and other communities in the Puget Sound-Seattle/King County area of Washington State that have historically faced inequities, oppression, and lack of access. NAC's mission is to empower communities by building strong nonprofits and community leaders to shape institutions and policies to achieve social justice and equity. NAC influences and guides the practice of the nonprofit sector and other institutions through its technical assistance, training, leadership development, and community-based research and evaluation.

NAC began providing management/infrastructure development work seven years ago but quickly infused other community building and leadership development activities into the array of services provided. In addition to using culturally competent staff, consultants, and approaches, NAC staff reflect the diversity of NAC's constituents. Staff have relationships of reciprocal respect and trust within the communities NAC serves, and in many cases these relationships preceded their work with NAC.

PILA–Partnership for Immigrant Leadership and Action

2601 Mission Street, Suite 404
San Francisco, CA 94110

Phone: 415-821-4808
Fax: 415-821-4809
www.PILAweb.org

Originally founded in 1997 (and formerly known as NCCP), since 2000 PILA has been working to increase civic and political activism among low-income immigrant communities in order to strengthen democracy and advance social justice.

PILA's work is inspired by the immense contributions that these communities make to the economic, cultural, and spiritual fabric of our communities. We envision a place where all people, regardless of citizenship status, have full access to basic civil and human rights.

The organization pursues three key goals:

- *Increase the capacity of Bay Area organizations to develop grassroots immigrant leadership and involve immigrants in the electoral process*

- *Contribute to strengthening the fields of organizational capacity building, leadership development, and immigrant civic and voter participation across the country*

- *Develop and participate in strategic alliances that connect PILA's local work to broader impact, and support grassroots immigrant involvement in state and national policy formation*

RefugeeWorks

Lutheran Immigration & Refugee Services
700 Light Street
Baltimore, MD 21230

Phone: 410-230-2876
Fax: 410-230-2859
www.LIRS.org

As the National Center for Refugee Employment and Self-Sufficiency, RefugeeWorks strives to help newcomers achieve independence by providing resources, training, and expertise in refugee employment; sharing strategies and promoting promising practices throughout the refugee employment network; and offering a

forum for the analysis and airing of important issues that impact new arrivals. The program fulfills its mission through a variety of technical assistance channels, including trainings, consultations, and employment-related publications. Each year, RefugeeWorks organizes six two-day Employment Training Institutes for frontline service providers nationwide. The staff and peer experts also present at national and regional conferences on a near weekly basis. Services and resources extend to employment service providers— nonprofit organizations, governmental agencies, and other entities that work directly with refugee clients seeking employment. Established by Lutheran Immigration and Refugee Service (LIRS) in 1997, RefugeeWorks serves as the training and technical assistance arm of the U.S. Office of Refugee Resettlement.

United Way of Greater Toronto

26 Wellington Street East, 11th Floor
Toronto, Ontario M5E 1W9
Canada

Phone: 416-777-2001 x223
Fax: 416-777-0962
www.unitedwaytoronto.com

United Way of Greater Toronto (UWGT) is an incorporated nonprofit charity focused on improving the long-term health of our community. UWGT runs Canada's largest annual fundraising campaign, supporting 200 social service agencies that provide a vital network of assistance. We strive to multiply community impact through fund distribution, research and public policy, advocacy and convening, resource development, capacity building, and strategic initiatives.

A volunteer board of trustees of leading community members governs all United Way decision-making. The board oversees how donor money is used, shapes strategic vision and plans, and monitors organizational performance.

The Campaign Cabinet is the driving force behind the UWGT annual campaign. These business and community leaders meet with colleagues and peers to encourage the participation of their organizations in the United Way campaign. The Campaign Cabinet's effort ultimately involves 20,000 volunteers, and reaches into workplaces large and small across the city.

Authors of This Report

The authors of this report would like to thank our project advisors, William Yang, Jennifer Godinez, and Saeed Fahia, for their insight, patience and persistence through our journey.

Emil Angelica has over twenty-five years experience providing consulting and training services on board and staff development, strategic planning, finance, organization development, program evaluation, policy and community development, and nonprofit management. He has worked on a broad range of mergers and collaborations, including projects for refugee and immigrant communities. Emil has directed a nonprofit organization. He has authored books on management and is a national speaker and trainer. Emil has degrees in finance, management, and philosophy.

Vicki Asakura is the executive director of the Nonprofit Assistance Center. Vicki, a third generation Japanese American and a Seattle native, has thirty years experience planning and managing programs serving refugee/immigrants, including culturally competent capacity building and leadership development. She was instrumental in organizing the first Refugee Community Building Conference, now a statewide event. She is the current chair of the King County Refugee Planning Committee, a community driven advocacy and planning body for refugee services.

Hilary Binder-Aviles coordinates Mosaica's capacity building assistance to community-based organizations, and is a cofounder of Sol & Soul, a Washington, DC-based arts and activism organization. Many generations removed from the immigrant experience of her German, French, and English ancestors, Hilary began 'crossing borders' as a college student, working with Vietnamese refugees in Massachusetts. She lives with her husband Quique, who is originally from El Salvador, and her dog Zapata, who will lead the canine revolution.

Barbara W. Fane is training and technical assistance (TA) manager at the Nonprofit Assistance Center. Her work focuses on organizational capacity building, including training, TA services, regranting process, and managing a consultant network. Barbara has worked with refugee and immigrant communities for more than fifteen years. She has a strong affinity for the refugee experience as an American of primarily West African descent whose ancestors were inhumanely transported, without choice, to America via the Western enslavement experience.

Anushka Fernandopulle provides consulting, training, and research services at CompassPoint in the areas of staff management, strategic planning, executive transitions, and board development. Anushka's approach has been influenced by nonprofit work focused on public health, youth, immigrants, and refugees, as well as a degree in social anthropology from Harvard University and an MBA in nonprofit management from the Yale School of Management. Anushka's family immigrated to the United States from Sri Lanka shortly before her birth.

Sarah Gleason is a consultant on staff at Fieldstone Alliance. She is the project manager for the Nexus Project. Sarah works primarily as a trainer and facilitator, in the areas of civic engagement, leadership development, and cultural diversity. Sarah is also involved in faith-based social justice organizing. She has worked in a number of French-speaking African countries, and her spouse is West African. Sarah herself is a Minnesotan of European descent.

Cheryl Hamilton is the national coordinator for RefugeeWorks at Lutheran Immigration and Refugee Service (LIRS). In her role, she delivers trainings across the country on topics related to refugee employment and self-sufficiency. She also has significant experience collaborating with various organizations and government programs on cultural integration and secondary migration issues. A granddaughter of Irish and French-Canadian immigrants, Cheryl was raised in Maine.

Monica Herrera is an immigrant from Chile. She arrived in Minnesota in 1967 with her parents and three sisters and settled into a small suburb in Minneapolis. When a military coup d'etat occurred in the early 1970s, the family decided to make Minnesota their permanent home. Monica's professional experiences have been spent between the nonprofit and public sector with a common theme of working to address issues of access and equity for women and children.

Barbara Jeanetta, on the staff of Twin Cities LISC, is responsible for capacity building efforts with community-based and emerging developers from new immigrant and communities of color. Her background is in management and administration of nonprofits and local government. Barbara lives on the West Side of St. Paul, a gateway community for many immigrant and refugee groups. Her mother is a first generation immigrant and Barbara grew up in a large, Italian-speaking extended family.

Sida Ly-Xiong is a research and consulting associate with Fieldstone Alliance. Her work in the nonprofit and government sectors has included creating youth leadership programs for immigrant and refugee communities in Wisconsin; researching community development and environmental management initiatives in Botswana; and mediating dispute resolutions for the State of Minnesota. Sida is Hmong and was born in a refugee camp in Thailand. Her family was sponsored by a Catholic community in Wisconsin, where she grew up.

Amanuel Melles has been involved in community development in Canada and Eritrea since 1982. He is the director of Organizational Capacity Building with the United Way of Greater Toronto. Amanuel has a wide range of expertise within the human services sector. In 2001 and 2002 he was publicly recognized for ideas and insight that support the diversity of urban life. Prior to coming to Canada, he enjoyed teaching and researching at the University of Asmara, Eritrea.

Heba Nimr is a program director at PILA—Partnership for Immigrant Leadership and Action. She is the daughter of immigrants from Palestine and Egypt. She was born and raised in an upper middle class household in Toledo, OH. She has more than fifteen years experience working and volunteering with various organizations and projects based in or serving diverse immigrant communities in the Midwest, East Coast, and Northern California. She also has significant experience working with social justice organizations where the primary constituencies are not necessarily recent immigrants.

Ann Philbin is one of three founders and codirectors of the Center to Support Immigrant Organizing, where she has worked for the last six years. Previous to her work at CSIO, Ann lived and worked long term outside of the United States on two occasions, once in Central America and once in East Central Europe. For four years, she was the director of an immigrant worker support center in the Boston area. Ann is of Irish-American descent and is fluent in Spanish.

Anne Pyke is senior manager of education and resource development in the Organizational Capacity Building Unit (OCB) at United Way of Greater Toronto (UWGT). In 1999, recognizing the strength of Toronto's ethno-racial diversity, UWGT adopted a new priority area for funding and capacity building, called Helping Newcomers Fulfill their Potential. Anne has worked under this priority in teaching, training, leadership, and strengthening the organizational capacity of organizations serving immigrants and refugees in suburban areas of Toronto.

Charley Ravine has served as MAP for Nonprofit's legal and human resources director since 1983. He has served on a number of nonprofit boards and committees, including Senior Community Services and Jewish Family & Children's Service. During his tenure at MAP, Charley has provided direct assistance in incorporation and application for exempt status with over five hundred organizations, including in recent years many immigrant- and refugee-led organizations from Southeast Asia, East Africa, West Africa, and Eastern Europe.

Monica Regan is a program director at PILA—Partnership for Immigrant Leadership and Action, where she has worked for six years to develop innovative capacity building programs to strengthen immigrant civic and political activism. Raised in San Francisco in a large extended Irish Catholic family, Monica has also lived in Latin America and speaks Spanish. She has over thirteen years of experience working in diverse immigrant communities in Northern California and the Pacific Northwest.

Luz Rodriguez is a founder and codirector of the Center to Support Immigrant Organizing (CSIO), where she has worked for the last six years. Luz is an immigrant from Colombia and has been in the United States since 1989. When she first came to the United States, Luz worked as a cleaning worker. Since then, she has worked as a community and labor organizer, educator, legal services provider, and technical assistance provider for immigrant communities at several different organizations.

Alfredo Vergara-Lobo brings years of experience with nonprofit and public entities domestically and internationally to his work at CompassPoint Nonprofit Services. Alfredo received his MSW and BA from UC Berkeley and from San Francisco State University respectively. An immigrant from El Salvador, Alfredo has consulted with nonprofits and government entities in the areas of strategic planning and partnerships, board development, organizational development, and cultural competence. A popular speaker and trainer, Alfredo presents in both English and Spanish.

Printed in the USA
CPSIA information can be obtained
at www.ICGtesting.com
JSHW060048150824
68134JS00031B/2669

9 780940 069626